ALSO BY MARILYN PABON

Divine Feminine Handbook is a four-book series:

Volume I: Overcoming Self-Doubt

Your Divinity, your femaleness, and your self-worth, once revealed will wipe away any self-doubt you ever had about yourself. You will be fearless and never feel you have to bow down to anyone or feel second rate to anyone ever again.

Volume II: Unleash Your Inner Goddess

You know you are stepping into your Goddess-self and awakening your true eternal nature when you become more concerned about your inner journey more than your outward one.

Volume III: Extreme Feminine Self-Care

Extreme feminine self-care is attending to the needs of your whole being. Putting health and self-care at the heart of everything will allow you to enjoy reaping the endless benefits of a healthy body and a clear mind during the time you spend on Mother Earth.

Volume IV: Self-Reliance in a Changing World

Self-reliance does not mean being alone and carrying the weight of the world on your shoulders, it is about being responsible for your life and taking the lead when it comes to planning, making decisions, and taking the initiative to make certain things get done in a manner that is in your best interest.

Divine Feminine Handbook

Volume IV

Self-Reliance
In a Changing World

MARILYN PABON

BALBOA.PRESS
A DIVISION OF HAY HOUSE

Balboa Press books may be ordered through booksellers or by contacting:

Balboa Press
A Division of Hay House
1663 Liberty Drive
Bloomington, IN 47403
www.balboapress.com
844-682-1282

Because of the dynamic nature of the Internet, any web addresses or
links contained in this book may have changed since publication and
may no longer be valid. The views expressed in this work are solely those
of the author and do not necessarily reflect the views of the publisher,
and the publisher hereby disclaims any responsibility for them.

The author of this book does not dispense medical advice or prescribe the use
of any technique as a form of treatment for physical, emotional, or medical
problems without the advice of a physician, either directly or indirectly. The
intent of the author is only to offer information of a general nature to help
you in your quest for emotional and spiritual well-being. In the event you use
any of the information in this book for yourself, which is your constitutional
right, the author and the publisher assume no responsibility for your actions.

Any people depicted in stock imagery provided by Getty Images are
models, and such images are being used for illustrative purposes only.
Certain stock imagery © Getty Images.

Print information available on the last page.

ISBN: 978-1-9822-7511-2 (sc)
ISBN: 978-1-9822-7512-9 (e)

Balboa Press rev. date: 10/13/2021

INTRODUCTION

Divine Feminine self-reliance is more than being self-sufficient. It means not clinging to people. It means not making life harder for others than it already is. For the most part, it's an attitude, and it's one that will serve you well no matter the circumstances in which you find yourself.

You probably know someone who lives on their own terms, with an independent attitude and a determination to take care of their own needs, they are accountable for themselves. The shift to taking responsibility for our lives is vital to transforming our life into one of Divine Feminine self-reliance.

No matter what challenges we face we must learn to save ourselves. Do not wait for someone else to come along (the proverbial white knight). Do not buy into the old story that someone else can take better care of you than you can. Your Divine Feminine Power is all about being self-reliant.

Don't wait for someone else to appreciate you, love you, acknowledge you or save you. You are a Divine Feminine. Stand strong in knowing who you are. You are a wise soul with all the wisdom you needed to come to this earth for your own personal growth, and to fulfill your earthly mission. You are already wise, strong and independent or you wouldn't be here on your earthy journey.

When we think of self-reliance, sometimes we think of everything being on our shoulders. That's not the case. Being self-reliant and independent doesn't mean you have to be alone, it is being responsible for your life and taking the lead when it comes to planning, making decisions, and taking action. It's about you taking the initiative and making certain things get done in a manner that is in your best interest.

Being self-reliant is the only way to keep you and your family safer in our uncertain world. You can be truly happy, proud of yourself and live a fulfilling, purposeful life. This book will encourage and teach you to embrace a more self-reliant Divine Feminine mindset, one small step at a time in many areas of your life. Your Divine Feminine energy, power and intelligence to do so, is your wise soul's gift to yourself, and the planet.

CONTENTS

Section Two: Homemaking Skills

Section Three: Survival Skills

SECTION ONE

Divine Feminine Self-Reliance Skills

CHAPTER 1

Becoming A Self-Reliant Divine Feminine

Self-reliance and self-respect are the necessary keys most unhappy women need to grasp the concept of, while taking full responsibility for and control over their own lives. Until they find these keys, dissatisfied women dream that there is someone else out there who "can make it better", who can take total care of them, who can be responsible for them more effectively than they can for themselves. This condemns them to searching for the person who can protect them, care for them and control them. Self-reliance and happiness begins when:

- We realize how false and destructive this dream is
- When we understand that no one can take care of us better than we care for ourselves
- That only we are responsible for our lives
- We start to learn effective methods of doing things for ourselves

By developing self-reliance and independence, (which is the ability to take care of and be responsible for yourself), you acquire:

1. Emotional Competence

Emotional tools are necessary to free yourself from dependency. To be responsible is to be able to make effective decisions and choices for yourself. To weigh alternatives, and to evaluate ethical dilemmas and solve problems. When a problem arises, the independent woman has acquired the skills it takes to face it squarely, learns as much as possible about it, considers many options, weighs the possible outcome of each option, and perhaps seeks advice and counsel before reaching a decision. As an independent and self-reliant woman, you can ask directly for help, but you remain in charge of how much and what kind of help you accept, and you make clear agreements about what is expected in return.

2. Inner Role Model

When you develop self-reliance and independence with yourself, you also are developing the role models that enable you to choose appropriate friends and suitable mate. The interaction you have with yourself is a role model for all your other relationships. For example, if you criticize yourself frequently, you're more likely to stay around others who are critical, because it feels familiar.

Likewise, self-reliance and independence in yourself also helps you see it in others. When you have a caring, responsible relationship with yourself, you develop an internal relationship model to use as a basis for your friendships and intimate relationships with others. As you become more experienced at identifying healthy friendships, your circle of good friends grows, beginning with your relationship with yourself, expanding to a few new friends, and eventually growing into a supportive "family" of choice who reinforce your autonomy and independence.

3. Self-Understanding

You gain the understanding that you are responsible for yourself and must learn whatever you need to make your life successful, functional and happy; rather than waiting around for someone else, or trying to gain another's approval.

Taking care of and being responsible for yourself requires skills that are usually learned in early childhood. However, we don't always get the healthy positive examples we need, so we grow up without the necessary learning. This is not unusual, or entirely the fault of our parents. If you were gradually taught and encouraged to be self-reliant from early childhood, you would learn the necessary skills and attitudes for autonomous living one step at a time. Unfortunately for many of us, our parents were not trained in autonomy either, and could not teach us.

The popular idea of parents' "responsibility" for children can be counter-productive. Parents who see their role as controlling their offspring rather than teaching them to make choices on their won, teaches the children dependency and insecurity rather than independence.

Contrary to what you may think, self-reliance and independence actually enhance relationship with others, and allow giving and receiving to be truly unconditional. Only a woman who is truly fully able to care for herself can be free to love and give freely; deprived people give grudgingly.

4. You Don't Disregard Self-Care

When it comes to a healthy diet, proper exercise, and getting enough sleep, strong women prioritize these self-care activities.

Women who are independent realize they have to take care of themselves first, focusing on the nutrition and rest which their bodies need in order to function at an optimal level. They know when it is time to put their work aside to rejuvenate themselves, and they know how to stay in tune with their mental, physical, and emotional needs.

5. You Get An Education

It is common for women to forego an education to focus on maintaining a home and family. As women, our future is full of opportunities that we cannot currently imagine; the best way to prepare ourselves is to pursue an education, which has its own spiritual value regardless of whether we ever enter the paid labor force. Education does more than make a person marketable; education helps develop our spirits and our spiritual gifts.

A woman's education should prepare her for more than the responsibilities of motherhood. It should prepare her for the entire period of her life.

6. You Never Stop Learning

A self-reliant woman never believes that she knows enough. She never stops aspiring to learn about new things. She reads, keeps up with current events, scientific discoveries, and technological inventions, as well as her interests and hobbies.

7. You Aren't Reluctant To Invest In Yourself

You don't hesitant to invest your time or money into improving yourself. You know your value and understand that in order to help other people, you need to first help herself. Let us do all we can to invest in our potential, earthly and divine, so we may be ready for all life has in store for us.

8. **You Don't Wait For Permission**

If you want to do something, you don't wait for someone to tell you that you are allowed to do it. You makes well-considered choices that support your independence and inner strength.

You make your own decisions with confidence and do not need to consult a partner or a parent to know what is in your best interest. But you are smart enough to know when to communicate and compromise with the important people in your life about decisions that might affect them.

9. **You Don't Wait For Things To Find You**

If you want money, you get a job. If you want a family, you make one. If you want a partner, you find one. You don't wait around for someone to rescue you or tell you what to do. You know what to do and you do it. You are proactive, not reactive.

Many Areas Of Our Life That Require Self-Reliance

Divine Feminine self-reliance is more than being self-sufficient. It means not clinging to people. It means not making life harder for others than it already is. For the most part, it's an attitude, and it's one that will serve you well no matter the circumstances in which you find yourself.

You probably know someone who lives on their own terms, with an independent attitude and a determination to take care of their own needs, they are accountable for themselves. The shift to taking responsibility for our lives is vital to transforming our life into one of Divine Feminine self-reliance.

No matter what challenges we face we must learn to save ourselves. Do not wait for someone else to come along (the proverbial white knight). Do not buy into the old story that someone else can take better care of you than you can. Your Divine Feminine Power is all about being self-reliant.

Self-reliance will look different for different people depending on the stage of your life, where you live and your health. There are many areas of our life that require self-reliance.

Lifestyle

Self-confidence is defined by dictionary.com as "belief in oneself and one's powers or abilities; self-confidence; self-reliance; assurance."

Today's world is filled with opportunities, the more self-reliant and self-aware you are, the more certainty you will have. And when you have more certainty, you'll have more energy to work on what gives you inner satisfaction and take advantage of opportunities that align with your values.

When we think of self-reliance, sometimes we think of everything being on our shoulders. That's not the case. What we're really talking about is you being responsible for your life and taking the lead when it comes to planning, making decisions, and taking action. It's about you taking the initiative and making certain things get done in a manner that is in your best interest.

Spiritual Self-Reliance

"People who truly understand what is meant by self-reliance know they must live their lives by ethics rather than rules." Wayne Dyer

Spiritual self-reliance is essential to our well-being. It allows us to follow our heart, it encourages us to listen to our intuition and do what is right for ourselves. It is about your ability to experience direct personal revelation. We seek our own experiences and do not rely on the experiences and stories of others. Spiritual self-reliance truly frees us to be the best we can be.

Education / Skills

There was a time when the majority of our ancestors created things with their own hands, for themselves and for those around them. There is a huge myth out there about self-reliance. Far too many people believe that it means you exist only on what your two hands can grow or create, that it means living without other people, and that you basically have to do everything yourself in order to be self-reliant. That is extreme, but you can make the way you live your life a revolutionary act by producing some of the things that you need.

Getting an education and trade skills will enable you to make the money you need to live the lifestyle of your choosing and provide for yourself and your family, without being dependent or a burden on others. Get an education in something you enjoy or are passionate about so that while you are earning a living you are also fulfilling your desire to better the world in your field of interest.

Employment

We become more self-reliant as we learn to love work and seek inspiration to find the best ways to provide for ourselves.

Even if your goal is to be a full time wife and mother and not a professional woman in the workforce, you need to have employable skills, whether or not you choose to use them. Life throws us curve balls, nothing is absolute. We need to prepare ourselves to be self-reliant in the event we choose to remain single or our partner becomes ill, disabled, dies or leaves.

The world has changed and gone are the days when women

didn't have to prepare to go into the work force, if even to supplement the families income or enjoy a hobby/side job to put away money in savings or go on vacations. Whether you are single or have a partner it is increasing more difficult to live well on one income.

Free Yourself From the Rat Race

Never before have we had entire cities full of people who clock in their hours at work, come home and then sit in front of mass entertainment while eating prepackaged and precooked food.

Self-reliance is a movement and idea that reminds us we are more than just dependent drones clocking in our hours. It reminds us that there is more to life than the rat race. It reminds us that we can still take back that control.

When you make lifestyle choices that remove your dependence on faceless corporations, no matter where you start, you are increasing your self-reliance.

Self-reliance is a revolutionary act these days. The biggest insurrection in our society is to be as self-sufficient as possible and not dependent on large corporations or the government.

Self-reliance is being able to think for yourself. It is much harder for governments and big business to control people who have common sense, think for themselves and make decisions in their best interest, which is their God given right.

Financial Self-Reliance

More people are deeply in debt more than ever, living a fancy lifestyle that would crumble with one missed paycheck. They are slaves and they don't even know it.

Being a self-reliant Divine Feminine also means being more

self-directed about your personal finances. I'm dedicated to frugal living, because it's in my best financial interest, and no one else has my best interest in mind better than I do. It surely isn't the banks who keep sending me credit card offers who hope I will take the bait and live beyond my means.

My Motto:

- Avoid debt
- Save money
- Less is sometimes more

The more self-reliant skills you have the more money you can save for:

- Making purchases without going into debt
- Emergencies
- Retirement
- Vacations and entertainment

Health Self-Reliance

You are a soul with a mortal body. Everything you truly are is not your body. The body is just how your soul is transported around. It's the vehicle to get your soul and our mind from place to place. It's the way you can express what you're feeling and thinking. It's like your soul and mind got into your body and decided to drive it around for a while.

If you have abused your body for years and keep doing it, the vehicle that carries you around is going to break down a lot earlier than it has to. You have to love yourself enough to not neglect your health. Every woman should be the queen of her own body.

You are in control of your life and responsible for the health of your body. You have more control over your health than most people are aware of. Your body has the ability to heal and repair itself if you give it what it needs and take away what is harming it. But it can also age quickly and deteriorate if it isn't cared for.

If meals are not planned, it will be easier to choose fast food and lounging on the couch in front of the TV instead of trying a new plant based recipe or going for a walk.

When you think about buying fresh organic fruits and veggies, and become discouraged thinking it is too expensive to eat healthy, you must realize that it's really expensive to eat unhealthy foods. You can't afford to eat unhealthy; it might just cost you your life.

If you think you don't have time and will get to it later and continue to neglect your health, then you might not have your health later. You could end up living the rest of your days in chronic pain, diseased and on medications. Maybe you do have the time after all, you just have to be a little creative and intentional.

Home Storage and Emergency Preparedness

There are many possible emergency situations we could find ourselves in and it is our Divine Feminine responsibility to prepare for the safety of ourselves and our families. It would not be very Divine to find yourself unprepared, helpless and at the mercy of others if it could have been prevented if you had cared enough to prepare a little bit.

Learning self-reliant homemaking skills, storing extra food and home goods, learning natural medicine and first aid skills, and putting money away in savings will go a long way if you should find yourself in a financial emergency or natural disaster.

Wise Self-Reliance

- As a strong Divine Feminine, independent woman, you are self-reliant and can do things on your own, but you also know when you need input, support, and partnership.
- You are strong enough to know when to step back and let someone else shine in the spotlight or take the reins without compromising yourself.
- When you plan your week, day, morning, afternoon, and evening in advance, you will find that you get more control of your time and self-discipline to do the things you didn't have time for before.
- You are wise enough to schedule fun-time into your schedule.
- Becoming this type of divine feminine woman may take time and practice. You may need to change your mindset, let go of some limiting beliefs, and take some risks.
- Examine where you need to become more independent in your actions, decisions, and ideas, and make small changes to reclaim your personal Divine Feminine self-reliant power.
- When we surrender to our imperfection, something magical happens; love and acceptance turns into poetry.

I encourage you to embrace a more self-reliant mindset, one small step at a time. Your Divine Feminine energy, power and intelligence to do so, is your wise soul's gift to yourself, and the planet.

CHAPTER 2

Self-Reliance in Intimate Relationships

*"You knew from the moment our eyes met that
I had the spirit of a warrior. It's not good enough
for me to just survive, I must overcome and thrive.*

*"I won't be denied what I pursue and
I don't know how to quit. There is no
such thing as half way in my world. Good
enough is something for someone else.*

*"You will always know where you stand with me
because my voice will always be heard. I will always
listen to my heart and march to my own beat.*

*"If you can't love me like an equal and treat
me with respect, then you need to look elsewhere.*

*"Don't treat me like an option
if you want to be a priority."*

First Things First

- While it makes sense when you're a child to rely on your parents for important decisions, once you become an adult, you should be able to be comfortable doing things by yourself.
- You don't have to have family, friends, or a significant other taking care of you, you can get a job, make your own money, and support yourself, you can be self-reliant and fabulous.
- Don't let yourself be taken care of, take care of yourself.
- You can be anyone you want to be once you become self-reliant and can take care of yourself, by yourself.
- Once you love yourself and prove that you're strong, then you can be a good friend, family member, and/or significant other.
- You Belong to Yourself Before You Belong to Anyone Else.

Dating problems?

When the right person comes into your life, it will be to enhance your already happy life, not to complete it. That's the healthy approach to dating. Dating problems begin to disappear when you overcome your insecurities and limiting beliefs about romantic relationships. There are fewer dating issues when you are self-confident, self-reliant and can communicate your wants and needs clearly and have self-respect. When you have a positive approach to dating, it's just a matter of time before you find someone special to enhance your already happy self-reliant life.

Don't Rush Into An Exclusive Relationship

Dating and friendships is not only fun and entertaining it is a necessary process of learning there are so many different personality types and lifestyles which are different from your own. This is a time when it is extremely important to love yourself and have enough self-confidence to be an open book and let others see exactly who you are and what you stand for. You want to attract a potential partner who will love you exactly as you are and understand from the get go they cannot mold you into something different, who they want you to be. If they don't love you as you are, they don't love you enough. They are not your person. This isn't the time to settle.

Proactive Strategy

While dating you're still in the building stage, expectations are there but it's easier to open up about issues that threaten difficulty. Learning how to talk through differences will form good habits and potentially carry you through years to come.

Be Authentic and Expect the Same in Return

When you meet someone you are crazy about you may be tempted to mold yourself into their world and who you think they want you to be, but this is a big mistake. Don't be an imposter. We are who we are and eventually will revert back to that person which will only disappoint the one you are trying to impress. We all tend to put our best selves out there when we are dating which is an important reason to get to know someone for a long time before getting involved in a committed relationship. You want to make sure you really know who you are getting involved with, their good and dark side.

Friends and Family

It is important that you and your potential partner both like each others family and friends. If you don't this is a big red flag for much conflict in the future. Couples may feel protective of their experiences growing up, with strong attachments to where they came from. There may be some work that needs to be done to find compromise if part of one's family is more involved than others. Conversations about boundaries and roles of each of the families are important. This issue can and should be a deal breaker from the start if you just don't like their friends and/or family and vice versa. You can only compromise so much and this issue will be a lifelong struggle.

Spirituality

What does spirituality mean to you? For many of us spirituality is a guiding force in our lives. You may have a different views about spirituality that needs to be discussed up front so you have an understanding where you each are is coming from. Ideas and beliefs can be very different even if you come from the same religious or spiritual background.

Past Relationships

Your past affects your future together. Its important to talk through your backgrounds because the dynamics of old relationships can unconsciously transfer into new ones. Talking about them allows you to be more conscious and make better choices.

Managing Conflict

You need to learn each others style of communication. If one partner is comfortable with appropriately expressed anger and to the other, anger is a four letter word, communication is going to be an issue. Some people are conflict avoiders and some are conflict approachers. Neither is right or wrong. Arguing about every little thing leads to a conflict filled relationship. And never arguing leads to built up resentments and a lack of learned skills. If a couple cannot freely discus any subject, no matter how personal or difficult, the relationship is in for a big struggle.

Reconnecting After A Fight

Learning how to come back together and shake off your differences after a rift is an essential skill many couples don't know how to do.

Are You Considering Marriage?

The decision to marry is one of the most important decisions you have in your lifetime. One in two marriages end in divorce, yet a stable happy marriage is one of the most important life objectives for 93% of Americans.

Marriage Commitment

Are you willing to do the work it takes to make a relationship work? Are you willing to commit your life to one person and forsake all others? Couples who are willing to make sacrifices for the sake of the marriage are significantly more likely to have lasting long marriages and decease their chances of getting divorced. Is your partner on the same page and at the same level of commitment?

Couples often don't have enough relationship education and examples of relationships set by parents and family members are not always ideal. You may have an idea of what marriage looks like and what it means to be a partner but your partner may feel very differently.

Questions To Be Resolved Before Marriage

- What marriage expectations and roles does each person expect the other?
- How do each of you see the structure of the marriage?
- Do you agree on the division of the household chores and responsibilities?
- How will you handle your relationship with your families?
- Should you do everything together or give each other space for personal friends and activities?
- Where will you live?
- Do you want children? When? How many? Parenting style? Will extended family be involved?
- Money management has a way of ruining marriages. Each person has their own relationship with money. Getting clear on each others past and present financial history and common future goals is imperative. There should be no secrets or shame around money in a healthy relationship.

How are you going to handle your finances; spending vs saving?

Pre-Marital Counseling

If you are planning a wedding in a house of worship, some synagogues and churches require pre-marital counseling. Even if it isn't required, for many couples pre-marital counseling can be a beneficial way to dig deeper into getting to know yourself and your partner, especially if you are having trouble working through the questions above and you don't have great family role models to give you guidance. Pre-marital counseling isn't because there are already problems, it is to help you prevent potential problems and misunderstandings.

Being open to counseling and getting a different perspective shows maturity and commitment to your desired union. If you are open to it but your partner isn't, they may not be open to counseling down the road when there are real problems in the relationship.

Healthy Partnerships

Intimacy serves to help illuminate parts of oneself never truly realized. Healthy partnerships bring out the best in people, because when they feel safe and loved, they are free to grow and explore who they are as human beings. Instead of depending on a partner, we need to seek interdependence. We must believe that we do not have to go through life alone.

If you have an issue with being overly self-reliant, you must remember that allowing yourself to depend on others can actually help you to develop your autonomy and strength. Over time, as you reveal vulnerability with your partner, you may realize there is nothing to be afraid of. Letting go of control, fear and other intense emotions helps to make relationships more solid. As you grow secure in the idea that others love you and will not let you go, you learn that independence and love do not need to exist on separate planes. When you depend on others, you are at your strongest.

Achieving Interdependence

- Remind yourself that it's healthy to accept help from others and is a sign of strength rather than weakness.
- Interdependence is what makes the difference between happy and unhappy partnerships. Self-reliance when taken to extremes can deprive you of love and nurturance. Even though it's hard, you need to embrace the idea that it's okay to show weakness and allow others to nurture you.
- Adopt a mindset that it's good to count on your partner. Believe that you can share your deepest feelings with them and it will promote healthy attachment, trust and intimacy. You must let them in and embrace the idea that you don't have to go through life alone.
- In relationships where partners do not offer mutual support, partners become disappointed in each other and come to believe that they must look out for themselves first. Mutual dependence is a trademark of a healthy relationship. Being able to give and take support is an essential ingredient in a successful relationship.
- Resist making big decisions without an enthusiastic agreement from your partner, especially important ones that impact both of you.
- Reigning in self-reliance will help you build a trusting relationship. When you first discover that your independent nature sometimes prevents you from true intimacy, you

may be unsure about how to change this pattern. It is often hard to decipher whether self-reliance is positive or negative. Becoming more conscious of your partner's needs and the value of mutual understanding is critical to developing lasting love.

- Many women struggle with being overly self-reliant and are fearful of depending on their partners for crucial support. This is the tragedy of the double-edged sword of reliance. On the surface, it's wonderful to be independent, self-sufficient and resilient. But when you believe you must do everything for yourself, you create your own demise. It's hard to let your partner in. It's hard to give them room to come through for you. But if you are ever to enjoy the full nature of intimacy, you must. In relationships small doses of self-reliance is positive.

Overcoming Disappointing Relationships

Many modern women are independent to a fault, putting far too much pressure on themselves. They bring self-reliance to a new level because they are unable to rely on anyone. Reliance on others can be healthy and affirming. The problem is that we may not have learned how to balance self-reliance with healthy interdependence.

Being self-reliant can serve us well as adolescents and single adults as we strive to achieve goals and a sense of identity. For instance, being raised in a divorced family and learning to be independent from a young age, can help to succeed at work and school. But as an adult, developing intimate relationships can be a challenge because it's not always easy to draw the line between being independent and relying upon your partner for emotional support.

Many women struggle with being overly self-reliant and are

fearful of depending on their partners for crucial support after seeing what happened to their moms who struggled financially after divorce. They feel like they never want to depend on anyone and have that happen to them. Raised by a single mom, they learn early of the risks of being too dependent on a partner.

Developing interdependence in a relationship is key to overcoming unhealthy self-reliance. While all relationships present us with risks, they are risks worth taking. You must surrender your shield and let others in, certain levels of dependence in intimate relationships can be beneficial and promote emotional closeness. There's a reason that a marriage is called a partnership. Despite the ease in which you can handle everything on your own, learning how beautiful it is to share the everyday burdens with someone else, even if it's just a stressful day, makes life delightful.

When Relationships End

No matter the circumstances, on some level, we blame ourselves when a relationship ends. We take it as a personal failure. The sorrow of heartbreak is not just about loss, but about self-doubt. When rejection is involved in the breakup, it triggers primal rage which we turn against ourselves, beating ourselves up.

We feel shame. We suddenly focus on all of our personal defects, believing that it was our lacking, inadequacies, faults, deficits, and negative behaviors that made us unworthy of someone's love. And somehow it is worse if the person was a smuck, because we think, "If the smuck didn't even want me, who will?"

The truth is that you don't have that much to do with how your partner behaves, whether they are faithful or stray, whether they stay or go, whether they treat you with respect or not, etc. They are going to do what they are gong to do, regardless of who their partner is. If your partner cheated on you, they would have cheated no matter who their partner was. If they abandoned you, they would have abandoned their partner no matter who she was. You can't take it personal. Sadly, as impersonal as it sounds, you have nothing to do with it, because that is just who they are. Those are their morales, values, or lack of integrity, again nothing to do with you. Stop blaming and shaming yourself.

Most people think too little of themselves and often falling in love is merely a compensation for inner emptiness, loneliness, and shame. No wonder most relationships fail.

Accept that now is the time to institute more self-love. Vow to stop laying your need for love and acceptance at your lover's feet, and take 100 percent responsibility to give yourself the love and esteem that you need (that's why they're called self-love and self-esteem).

Take advantage of this time of heightened insecurity to learn how to give yourself emotional security. Realize that it's nobody else's job, especially now that your lover has abdicated this role in your life. Only you can do this. You can survive on your own.

Don't wait for someone else to appreciate you, love you, acknowledge you or save you. You are a Divine Feminine. Stand strong in knowing who you are. You are a wise soul with all the wisdom you needed to come to this earth. You are already wise, strong and independent or you wouldn't be here.

Love is a Divine Feminine quality. Loving and nurturing yourself is a feminine quality all goddesses need to develop more. Nourish yourself daily with healthy activities; good nutrition, exercise, proper sleep, intimacy, and healthy interactions, with lots of time for fun, adventure, and relaxation.

The highest form of love is acceptance. Accept your humanness, flaunt your flaws; otherwise what you resist will persist. We transcend what we can graciously accept.

CHAPTER 3

Self Reliance In Your Wise Old Age

*When I get old, they're never going
to say, "What a sweet old lady."
They're going to say, "What
on earth is she up to now?!"*
Wild Woman Sisterhood

The Celtic tradition honors three passages in a woman's life; maiden, mother, crone. As crones we have integrated the tender aspects of the maiden, the many lessons of mothering and the rich experience of a life long lived. Still all are a part of the whole.

See your future self, a beautiful face graced with history, a healthy, vibrant body and a clear sharp mind. Trust this is the best time of life.

Old age is a great time to sit back and enjoy your life. You are much wiser, people's opinions do not easily fluster you, you are much more comfortable in your own skin. As you get older you will understand more and more that it's not about what you look like or what you own, it's all about the person you've become.

Enjoying your life is a significant contributor to healthy aging. A study conducted by researchers from the University College in London showed that happy people were more robust and fit.

The study followed older people aged 60 years and above living in England over the course of 8 years. This study examined the relationship between a positive outlook and physical well-being. It revealed that happy seniors had less trouble getting up, dressing, or taking a shower, as opposed to unhappy seniors who were twice as likely to develop diabetes, heart disease, cancer, and strokes. The enjoyment of life and general happiness are relevant determinants of mobility and future disability in seniors.

Stay Active

Exercise and physical well-being is a great place way to start. Exercising lifts your spirit and energy levels making you feel better. This is because your body releases feel-good hormones known as endorphins. Athletes refer to this feeling as the runner's high. Incorporating light workouts into your routine even if you did not exercise before reduces your chances of getting disabled by 25 percent.

Exercise also helps relieve chronic pain from conditions like arthritis and pinched nerves. It helps us maintain weight; therefore, preventing us from developing diseases such as obesity and diabetes, improves our metabolism, lowers blood pressure, and strengthens our immune system.

Eat Well

Eating a nutritious diet can be compared to physical activity in their importance to health according to a pyramid created for seniors by Tuft University researchers. Although your body is experiencing some changes, meal times can still be fun. Drink plenty of water to go on a high-fiber diet. Water is also suitable for healthy skin. Your diet should be a high-fiber diet (whole foods, nuts, fruits, and vegetables) and lean protein.

Be Stylish

Just because you are advancing in years should not mean that you can't do it in style. When you look good, you feel even better. Wear a hat and sunglasses to protect your skin, use retinoid creams on your face, drink plenty of water and indulge in a little makeup if you like that sort of thing. A great haircut can transform your face or even changing your hair color. A dark hair color makes your features look severe while a lighter skin tone softens them. If you have stained teeth, you can have them whitened in a short and simple procedure. Looking good will make you feel confident and fuel your purpose.

Moisturize Your Skin

Moisture, Moisture, Moisture. As we get older our skin loses it's elasticity. Mature women need to keep their hands, feet, face, and neck well moisturized. The most significant signs of aging are seen in our hands, around our eyes, and neck. Of course keeping your whole body moisturized is important as well.

Don't Isolate Yourself

Research has shown that a strong sense of purpose for seniors had a protective effect. People who stayed in touch with family and friends stayed healthy in their old age. A Gallup poll showed that seniors who spent hours daily being social were happier, enjoyed life, and were less likely to be stressed out or worried.

There is evidence that loneliness increases chances of depression and illness.

There has been a 50 percent increase over the last 15 years of people aged 55-64 years living alone and around one million people can go for 30 days without seeing anyone. Join clubs with activities that interest you or volunteer where you are likely to meet people who share your interests and values.

If you are single, widowed or divorced you could consider going on a date. There are dating websites for seniors to meet; you could also ask your friends to fix you up. Love is a beautiful thing and it's never too late. If you do not end up falling in love, you make a new friend, and it is still a win-win situation.

Reach Out

When a change occurs as it usually will, you will need a reliable support system. It could be a recent loss or a severe diagnosis. Working through your emotions by talking about them and listening to people who have been through similar experiences is soothing to the soul and will help you heal. While it is true that disability leads to depression, the inverse is also true, depression can lead to disability. That's why it is important to always reach out to someone and talk about your suffering.

Laugh A Lot

Laughing lowers the stress hormone cortisol. According to a study conducted, 20 minutes spent watching funny videos helped improve the memory in seniors. Some research also shows a link between happiness and lower risk of heart illness. So, laugh as much as you can because laughter really is the best medicine.

Read More

Keeping the brain stimulated which helps with connectivity helps keeps focus and attention. The more we read the more we expand our vocabulary and comprehension. Reading more as mature women allows us to relax and take a moment for ourselves. Therefore, reducing our stress and blood pressure. Opting to read keeps our mind focused on positive thoughts and feelings.

Occupy Your Mind

As we mature, keeping our mind occupied will eliminate boredom, anxiety, and depression. Because we're getting older, probably empty nesters, or kids are out with their friends, we end up with a lot of downtime. Having a hobby like gardening, knitting, sewing, or anything that requires you to be focused will help with those emotions that may come.

Relax

Take a day off to do nothing. Sleep in. Binge watch something on television. Be a bum for a day. Allow yourself permission to just be. Relieve the mind and body sometimes to let it recuperate. Take a day off to re-energize so you can keep going.

Stop Watching Television News

Learn about what is happening in the world on your own and form your own opinions sans commercial media. The less you allow others to interpret world events for you, the less you will be afraid of those events.

As we mature and grow certain things just aren't as important anymore. We become more calm, reserved, and life's intangibles become a priority. Don't look at maturing in a negative manner. Instead embrace it, have fun, and be grateful you made it thus far.

Teach, Inspire, and Motivate

Wisdom is the crown of the crone. Encourage and motivate the younger ladies. Because we have experienced life more and went through some storms, it's important to educate the younger ladies on the obstacles they may face. Giving back with wisdom and lessons you learned on the way will be more appreciated than you expect. Motivate and inspire a younger lady to go after her dreams. Uplifting someone else is free to do with a priceless reward.

Get A Dog

If you live alone you need a pet to love and keep you company. Dogs give you unconditional love, they are good company, good listeners and quit entertaining. They keep you busy and force you to care for something; you feed them, brush them, bathe them, train them and take them on walks. Holding them, petting them and talking to them is very calming and soothing to your soul.

Dogs are God's gift to humans. They will be your best friend, comfort you and make you laugh. Dog spelled backwards is God.

Have a Garden

Tending to a garden in the sunshine and fresh air is satisfying and rewarding. Spending about 30 minutes in the sun can provide you with nearly a day's supply of vitamin D through skin absorption. Having enough vitamin D in your body helps your bones form properly, which reduces your risk of developing bone diseases such as osteoporosis.

Soaking in daylight for at least 15 minutes at the same time every day, particularly in the morning hours, helps your body shut off a snooze-inducing chemical called melatonin. This will help your body develop a more stable night time and day time clock so you're less likely to have trouble sleeping when the sun goes down.

Open Your Windows

Getting more fresh air results in getting more oxygen into to the lungs helping airways to more fully dilate and cleanse your lungs. The brain needs 20 percent of the body's oxygen. More oxygen brings better clarity to the brain and improves concentration.

The Gift Of More Time

Since 1900, we've been gifted 30 extra years, 15 of which are likely to be productive and generative. You don't have to work until your final days, but you also don't have to disappear into obscurity or feel irrelevant. Because of this additional time, you get another chance to reinvent yourself and have time to do what's best for you.

CHAPTER 4

Divinely Living With Less

The amount of stuff we own these days is staggering. 90% of our purchases are trashed within 6 months.

The average American home size has grown from 1,000 square feet to almost 2,500 square feet. Personal storage generates more than $24 billion in revenue each year. Reports indicate we consume twice as many material goods today as we did 50 years ago. All while carrying, on average, nearly $15,950 in credit-card debt.

These numbers should cause us to start asking some difficult questions of ourselves. For example, "Why do we buy more stuff than we need?" What thinking would compel somebody to spend money they don't have on things they didn't actually need in the first place?

We buy bigger houses, faster cars, cooler technology, and trendier fashion hoping we will become happier because of it. Unfortunately, the actual happiness derived from excess physical possessions is fleeting at best.

Mindful Purchases

Digital marketing experts estimate that most Americans are exposed to around 4,000 to 10,000 ads each day. Quieting the voice of consumerism happens before you step foot in a store, opening a shopping app, or getting online. It happens when you look at your priorities for yourself, your money, and your home.

The first thing you have to do when you decide to live a more divine simple life is to determine what that means to you. One person's definition of simple living can be the polar opposite of what someone else thinks. Your life is yours, and you need to live a lifestyle that's fit for you. Keep in mind, living with less can be your passport for doing more. Minimalism is about clearing the clutter in our homes, calendars and heads so that we can do things that light us up and give us purpose.

Think about what you want in your day-to-day life. Do you want to save money? Live more minimally and organized? Zero waste? Live in a de-cluttered home? Spend more time with family? Work less and travel more? Lighten your load and have more fun?

We mistakenly look for confidence in the clothes we wear or the car we drive. We seek to recover from loss, loneliness, or heartache by purchasing unnecessary items. We seek fulfillment in material things. We often try to impress other people with the things we own rather than the people we are.

Trying To Fill The Void

Excess material possessions do not enrich our lives. They put us in debt, clutter our homes and use up our time as we work more to pay it off, clean it, take care of it, store it and organize it all.

British research found that the average 10 year old owns 238 toys and plays with just 12 of them daily. Excess consumerism starts at a young age as we are bombarded with advertising that tells us buying their products will make us happy.

If you've ever said "I have a closet full of clothes but nothing to wear", it's time to make some changes. Can you imagine the money you spent on clothes and shoes you only wore once or never and the books you haven't read and the beauty, diet and exercise products you never or rarely used? All of those excess "things" use to be your hard earned money in the bank.

Sensible Wardrobe

Begin With an Organized Sensible Wardrobe:

I think clothing is something that most of us Divine Feminine seem to accumulate a lot of without being mindful of what we actually wear.

- Decide to create a wardrobe you love.
- Keep only the comfortable items, and the ones that fit and you feel great in, because everything else is just taking up room.
- Letting go can be hard. Rather than asking yourself "What can I get rid of?" Ask, "What do I need to keep?" Of course you have things you want to keep that you may not need or have to have and that's ok, absolutely keep what you love.
- Match up your outfits and coordinate your colors and see what is left over.
- Look at an item and ask yourself; "If I saw this in the store today would you buy it?"
- Try on every pair of shoes. Are they comfortable? Are they still in style? Do you have anything to wear them with?

You will clear out more of your closet with this approach

rather than fretting over thinking you have to give up some of your clothes.

Use the same mind set in other areas of your home:

- Your linen closet; how many towels do you really need, sets of sheets, blankets, etc.
- Your kitchen; how many mugs and glasses and utensils, and table cloths do you really need?
- Your junk drawer; is it really junk or useful odds and ends?

CHAPTER 5

DIY Beauty and Home Care Products

Are you trying to live a healthier life, a more frugal life, a more self-reliant life? Learn to make your personal care and cleaning products using simple natural ingredients. You can create your own favorite products without the extra chemicals and save some money.

As with anything worth doing, it takes time, but considering that the skin is the largest organ of the body, and it absorbs the bad with the good, it's well worth taking time experimenting with formulas that work for you.

Personal Care Products

Our relationship to beauty products says so much about ourselves:

- Do we spend a fortune on tubes smaller than our pinkies that promise to erase any proof that we once smiled?
- Have we been buying the same stuff, month in, month out, since age fifteen?

- Do we follow the magazine reviews and share in the enthusiasm for this or that new molecule?
- Do we lose sleep over sulphates, chlorides, glycerines, and nano-particles ?
- Do we go full granola and make our own?

Store-bought skin care products are loaded with chemicals and can be downright expensive. In fact, many department-store and drugstore brands of skin care products are packed full of harsh chemicals, toxic ingredients, artificial colors and more. Even so-called natural skin care brands may contain questionable ingredients that you wouldn't want on your face.

We all use personal care products from shampoo to deodorant. They are an everyday staple for our families but, commercial products have plenty of down sides. From the cost to chemicals, personal care products can do more harm than good. Now you have options. Many personal care products can be made at home for pennies on the dollar without harmful ingredients like phosphates and aluminum.

By making products like body lotions and scrubs you eliminate many harmful fragrances, preservatives, and artificial ingredients. DIY versions of products you use daily, contain only what you place in them and are far less likely to irritate or flair up allergies because you can avoid ingredients you react to.

Products like toothpaste and mouthwash go directly into your body. Even if you spit it out you still ingest a fair amount of chemicals. Many chemicals in products you use daily lead to bad health and even cancer. By going natural you help keep your body healthy.

There are many ways to nurture your skin and hair, from a simple homemade face mask to scalp massages.

I'll be honest, getting started with homemade beauty products can be expensive at first, but once you build your apothecary these products are much cheaper to make than to buy.

Coconut Oil

This ingredient is always in my cabinet since we use it for cooking as well as a moisturizer. Coconut oil is antimicrobial and can help keep homemade beauty products fresh for a long time. I buy large jars of organic coconut oil at a local grocery store.

Cocoa Butter

Cocoa butter is super moisturizing and is hard at room temperature which makes it a great choice for lotion bars or other homemade beauty products that need some firmness.

Olive Oil

Though any liquid oil will do, I like olive oil because it's quite moisturizing and I already have it in my pantry. (I only buy organic, extra virgin, California olive oil since many others are fake).

Beeswax

Beeswax is very protective and moisturizing. Beeswax helps add a tad of stiffness to a product.

Grape Seed Oil

Grapes Seed oil is a great carrier oil for essential oils, it is moisturizing without being sticky.

Essential Oils

Whether you use them medicinally or just for the scent they impart, organic therapeutic grade essential oils are a great addition to any homemade beauty product.

Dried Herbs

If you're not into using essential oils medicinally, or you're not able to afford the ones you need yet, dried herbs are a great alternative. I like to make an herbal oil and use that in place of plain olive oil. Herbal oil will impart the medicinal qualities of the herb into the product as well as a mild scent. I try to grow as many herbs as I can.

Recipes for natural beauty products are ideal for anyone who has allergies or very sensitive skin, or for anyone who prefers using pure and natural products. Ingredients such as avocados, cucumbers, lemons, honey, and oatmeal give women absolute control over what they use on their bodies.

The following are an array of recipes to peak your interest and get you started experimenting. Always use organic ingredients whenever possible.

Ingredient Benefits:

Baking Soda: Gets rid of dirt, grime, pollution and excess sebum from deep within the pores. Unclogs pores hence preventing pimples.

Honey: Cleanses skin and removes excess sebum. Destroys germs that cause acne. Moisturizes oily skin.

Lemon Juice: Natural astringent. Has disinfecting properties that kill off acne causing germs on the skin's surface which prevents breakouts on oily skin. Lemon juice is effective against spots and freckles.

Coffee: has astringent and antioxidant properties, tightens and tones the skin. Coffee helps to cleanse, exfoliate and moisturize the skin making it an excellent face mask. The anti oxidants in coffee helps to firm and tighten the skin.

Milk: is antimicrobial/ cleansing properties.

Cocoa Powder: softens the skin/antioxidant properties.

Looking for a good facial scrub/exfoliate? Take a lemon, cut it in half. Dip one half in sugar, then scrub your face and lips.

Recipes

3 Ingredients Custom Face Oil

I make 4oz at a time. In the bottle I wish to use, I fill it up between 1/2 & 3/4 of the way with argan oil. Then, I pour in the rosehip oil, pouring in enough to almost fill the bottle. Then, I add lavender oil to finish filling the bottle (about 1 heaping teaspoon per 4oz).

I adore the combination of argan oil, rosehip oil, & lavender oil (fabulous for anti-aging!) but here's some other suggestions for you to use to make your very own custom face oil.

1st Ingredient: Base Oil

(Fill up your bottle between 1/2 & 3/4 full with this)

- Argan Oil: great for anti-aging – perfect for all skin types, including acne prone skin
- Jojoba Oil: great for anti-aging – perfect for all skin types, including acne prone skin (you can use half argan & half jojoba)
- Sweet Almond Oil: great oil for all skin types, but takes a lot longer for your skin to absorb
- Apricot Kernel Oil: best for normal, dry, and aging skin – not the best for acne prone
- Grapeseed Oil: good for oily, normal or acne-prone skin. Not the best for dry skin
- Avocado Oil: best for dry and aging skin
- Hemp Seed Oil: great light oil that's good for any skin type

2nd Ingredient: Nourishing Oil

(Add second, filling up the bottle to almost full)

- Rosehip Oil: best for regenerating skin cells and is known for it's firming/anti-aging abilities. Best for dry, normal, and aging skin
- Tamanu Oil: best thing to use for acne prone skin, oily skin, and scarred skin
- Borage Oil: really high in oleic acid, best for oily and acne prone skin
- Evening Primrose Oil: good for all skin types – can also be taken internally for acne prone skin
- Neem Oil: fabulous for oily and acne prone skin

3rd Ingredient: Essential Oil

(Top off your nearly full bottle with this, you don't need much)
- Lavender: great oil for all skin types – healing and calming
- Chamomile: great for all skin types, very healing
- Rose: absolutely incredible for aging skin, but expensive
- Palmarosa: great for acne-prone skin and aging skin
- Lemongrass: brightening and toning – best for normal, oily, or acne prone skin
- Rosemary: best for oily acne-prone skin

Instructions:

- Pour your 3 chosen ingredients into a 4ounce bottle.
- Tighten the lid and shake up to mix.
- Use morning and night on a clean face.

Coconut Oil Facial Scrub

Using equal parts of baking soda and coconut oil creates the perfect exfoliating homemade facial scrub.

Ingredients:

- 2 tsp. baking soda,
- 2 tsp. coconut oil

Instructions:

- Make into a paste, this is enough for your neck and face and maybe a little extra for the back of your hands.
- Scrub gently in circular motions for 3 min.
- Rinse with cold water.
- Your face may seem oily afterward, but within a few minutes the oil is absorbed and your skin is glowing.

I immediately saw a difference. Smaller pores and glowing skin! And the coconut oil moisturizes your skin for you. I use this scrub of baking soda and coconut oil every few days.

Fix Those Flaky Spots Mask

Have you ever noticed those flaky patches on your skin, especially your nose?

Ingredients:

Mix together:
- 2tbs of Sugar
- 1tbs of Honey
- 1tsp of Olive Oil

Instructions:

This mixture removes all the dead skin with the sugar, and the honey and olive oil will nourish your skin to the fullest, no matter the skin type. Just be careful to scrub gently.

Lemon and Egg Facial

Have red splotchiness on your face?

Ingredients:

- 1 egg yolk
- juice of 1 lemon

Instructions:

- Soothe symptoms away easily by mixing together one egg yolk and the juice of one lemon into a paste.
- Cover your face with it and leave it on overnight. If this seems like too much work, leave it on your face for an hour. You might not get the optimal results with this amount of time, but you will see a difference.

5 Minute Face Lift

This has a tightening effect and will leave your face fresh and glowing.

Ingredients:

- 1 egg white
- 1 tsp. fresh lemon juice

Instructions:
- Separate egg white into a small bowl
- Whip it up into a froth with a fork
- Add lemon juice and continue to whip to thicken
- Apply all over your face with your fingers
- Leave on for 5 minutes then wash off.

Insect Protection Oil

Contributed by Tanna Orr
This body spray keeps away tics, lice and mosquitos.

Ingredients:

- 1/4 cup grape seed oil
- 12 drops clove essential oil
- 12 drops lemon essential oil
- 10 drops rosemary essential oil
- 10 drops cinnamon essential oil
- 6 drops eucalyptus essential oil

Instructions:

- Using a small funnel add all ingredients to a small, clean spray bottle.
- Screw on the spray cap and shake vigorously until well blended.
- Store bottle in cool dark place when not in use.
- Blend will last 6 months to a year.
- Take it with you on your outdoor adventures.

Spray Deodorant with Magnesium

Low magnesium levels in the body have been associated with body odor. It is estimated that over 80% of us are deficient in this mineral. Magnesium oil in this deodorant recipe absolutely decreases armpit odor no matter how much you sweat.

Ingredients:

- 2 oz glass spray bottle
- Pinch of sea salt
- 15 drops lavender essential oil

- 5 drops frankincense essential oil
- 1 tablespoon magnesium oil
- Witch hazel

Instructions:

- In a small spoon combine the pinch of salt and the essential oils
- Place salt/oil mixture in your glass spray bottle
- Add the magnesium oil
- Fill the rest of the bottle with witch hazel.
- Shake and spray
- This deodorant has a shelf life of about 6 months

Home Cleaning Products

The cost of housecleaning products is equally as staggering. However, rather than spend a huge portion of your paycheck on cleaning products, you can simply use a few common items that you may already have around your house to create your own solutions.

You'll appreciate these DYI cleaners for several reasons:

- They work.
- They are inexpensive to make.
- They are natural.
- They make little or no waste.
- Since you probably have many of the items in the house, you don't need to buy much.

Before getting started, be prepared to label all of your homemade cleaners, including the ingredients you have used. While these products are mostly safe, you'll want a point of reference should a child or pet accidentally get into it.

Baking Soda

Baking soda is a hardworking cleaning item that is both versatile and very inexpensive.

Distilled White Vinegar

Like baking soda, distilled white vinegar is both versatile and inexpensive, and it can be used as a nontoxic disinfecting agent. Anytime "vinegar" is referred to throughout these tips, it's safe to assume that I'm referring to distilled white vinegar unless otherwise specified.

Hydrogen Peroxide

You might already have this in antiseptic solution in your medicine cabinet. If not, swing by the local drug store.

Cotton Balls

Supermarkets, drugstores, and dollar stores all carry large packs of cotton balls. If you're paying more than three or four pennies per cotton ball, you're probably paying too much.

Liquid Dish Soap

You probably already have liquid dish soap, but you might want to stock up on a bit more if you're using it for multipurpose cleaning solutions. There's no need to buy a fancy brand.

Salt

Chances are, you don't keep salt with your cleaning supplies. However, you might want to start doing so. Any table salt will do, though a coarser salt (like sea salt) is a good option.

Lemon

Pick up a lemon the next time you're at a grocery store, typically for less than a dollar.

Cheap Vodka or Rubbing Alcohol

If you're over the age of 21, consider purchasing a bottle of inexpensive vodka to keep with your cleaning supplies (and out of reach of children, just like with the rest of your cleaning supplies). If you're under 21 or aren't comfortable having vodka in your home, rubbing alcohol is a great substitute.

Corn Starch

A tablespoon of corn starch can be used in a glass cleaning solution.

Tea Tree Oil

Tea tree oil has microbial properties that make it an effective cleaner.

You also need some basic cleaning supplies:

- Nylon Scrub Brush
- Microfiber Cleaning Cloths
- Spray Mop
- Spray Bottles. You can reuse these bottles indefinitely, just remember to keep refilling it with the same solution. You don't want to accidentally mix a new solution with residue that was previously in the bottle and risk creating a toxic blend.
- Pumice Stone. Pumice stones are used to help break down and remove tough mineral deposits and stains. You may also recognize them from the nail salon if you

get pedicures. While not a "must-have" item, a pumice stone can help with stubborn stains, particularly in your bathroom and hard water stains in the toilet.

- You're also going to need a bucket and towel, as well as some water.

Recipes

Mirror Cleaner

I love cleaning with this, just so I can smell it. The hardest part is deciding which oil to choose, they all smell so good.

This mixture not only cleans the mirror (and faucets) to a shine, but because of the essential oils, it will help to prevent fogging while the shower is running.

Ingredients:

- 1 cup white vinegar
- 1 cup water
- 8 drops citrus oil (Lemon, Wild Orange, Lime, Grapefruit)

Instructions:

- Combine all ingredients in a spray bottle and shake well before use.
- Spray solution onto mirror and wipe with a dry cloth or towel.

Dryer Sheets

Simple, fast and makes clothes smell great.

Supplies:

- Small glass spray bottle
- 10 - 25 drops of your favorite essential oil
- water
- wash cloth

Instructions:

- Drop 10 to 25 drops of essential oil in a small spray bottle
- Fill with water and shake up
- Liberally spray on a wash cloth
- Put the cloth in the dryer with wet clothes

Laundry Scent Booster

Ingredients:

- 1 1/2 cup Epsom Salt
- 1/2 cup baking soda
- 20-30 Drops Essential Oils of choice

Instructions:

- Mix together all the ingredients listed above. Then, whisk together until all ingredients are well combined.
- Store in an air tight container.
- Add one scoop, about 1/4 cup, of the scent booster into the washer before adding any laundry. Add laundry and the normal amount of laundry detergent.

Notes:

- Laundry scent booster doesn't need to be added to every load, it can be used for those extra stinky, dirty loads. I personally choose to use it for each load.
- Make a double or triple batch to prevent having to make it so often if you do a lot of laundry.
- The shelf life is one year, but it never last that long in our home.
- To keep your laundry smelling great, add several drops of essential oils to a dryer ball and toss it in the dryer with

the laundry. I use the same essential oil that I use in my scent booster.

Laundry Scent Combos:

Fresh Citrus

- Lemon + Grapefruit + Orange + Tangerine + Mandarin + Spearmint
- Lemon + Basil
- Lemon + Clove + Grapefruit
- Wild orange + Tangerine + Bergamot
- Spearmint + Orange
- Bergamot

Freshly Clean

- Cedarwood + Lemongrass + Grapefruit
- Lavender + Eucalyptus
- Eucalyptus + Rosemary + Tea Tree
- Rosemary + Orange Rosemary + Lavender Rosemary + Peppermint
- Peppermint + Orange + Lavender
- Rosemary

Hard Water / Soap Scum Remover

Is your shower door covered in hard water stains?

Ingredients:

- 1 cup Epsom Salt
- ½ cup baking soda
- 1/4 cup liquid dish soap

Supplies:

- small bowl
- spoon
- sponge scrubber

Instructions:

- In a bowel mix ingredients with a spoon into a paste.
- Best when used right away. Mix up as needed.
- Scrub shower walls and doors with the paste and sponge.
- Requires a lot of rinsing but works better than store bought hard water cleaners.

CHAPTER 6

Meat and Vegetarianism During a Crises

The worldwide crisis caused by the COVID-19 virus has led to a renewed interest in backyard gardening, with seed sales spiking over 250% in March of 2020. Many people were concerned that not only would food supply chains remain stressed, but also that future food shortages would occur due to a lack of available farm workers who pick the crops.

The COVID-19 pandemic was a significant wake-up call to a lot of people. Anyone who was complacent in their emergency planning or simply "knew" the stores would always have what they needed were shaken up in a big way. Perhaps that describes you, or maybe you simply want help preparing for future supply disruptions on the horizon. Either way, we can take our cue from something our grandparents worked on 80 years ago: victory gardens (survival gardens).

Why Grow a Victory Garden?

Victory gardens were fruit, vegetable, and herb gardens planted at home during World Wars I and II. They were used by residents all over the world including in the United States, UK, Canada, Australia, and even Germany. They were designed to supplement rations and boost morale. Whenever the supply chain is disrupted, having your own victory garden can help you keep fresh food on the table and give you concrete ways to control supplies.

Seed Shortage

Beans: If for some reason there are no seeds to be found, you can also plant a variety of items found in your kitchen cupboard. I'm not kidding! Dry beans, including pinto and black bean varieties, usually are also viable seeds that can be planted. As the bean plant grows, it will eventually flower and produce young green bean pods, which can be harvested to cook as you would any green beans.

They are a delicious variety to eat green and can also be allowed to grow to maturity. When the husks are dry, one can harvest dry pinto beans, which can be cooked by boiling or placed in a pressure cooker. For a food source that is more practical, however, I recommend that you harvest the beans green, since they will produce even more after each picking.

Coriander Seeds: Another common spice rack item, coriander seeds, are what cilantro is grown from. Most will germinate and sprout within about a week. Plant cilantro or coriander seeds about 4" apart and keep the soil moist. Cilantro is a delicate and flavorful green that is often used in Mexican dishes such as tacos.

Red Pepper Seeds: Red pepper seeds, such as the ones found in a regular delivery pizza, also will germinate if they have not been crushed or cooked. You can grow pepper plants and have spicy red peppers in just over two months from the seeds that you find in your pizza box! Peppers, along with green beans and tomatoes, prefer sunny areas with well-draining soil.

Tomato Seeds: If you still have fresh tomatoes in your fridge, or received a take-out hamburger, look for gelatinous looking seeds inside. These can be placed in a dry spot for a couple days, then planted in soil to grow tomatoes. Even some kinds of sun-dried tomatoes (if they have not been heavily salted), may still contain viable seeds. Wash the dried tomatoes and let them soak in water and try to extract any seeds that you may find. Put them in a dry place for a couple days before placing in moist soil and see what happens. You will probably not have any luck from canned tomatoes, since cooking destroys the seed.

Potatoes: Russet and new potatoes will send out sprouts or "eyes" just before they spoil. If you have any potatoes that are "growing eyes," then simply cut off the growth, along with a bit of the potato, and plant the cuttings about 2" deep in loose soil in your yard. The potato plant will begin to grow out of the soil, while young potatoes grow in the soil underneath.

A large part of your survival garden should include options that are delicious to eat in their raw form. Most of the time, the raw version of a fruit or vegetable provides us with the highest nutritional content. This is not the case for all vegetables because some, like potatoes, cannot be eaten raw. In times of crisis, you might not have the means or time to cook your food and may have to resort to a few raw meals. Keep your options open for such circumstances.

Anything that is "wasted," whether it be because the leaves of a certain vegetable don't get used or a vegetable got rotten, should be recycled in your compost bin. The compost will eventually be used as soil and it will refresh your garden with many more nutrients which will help your plants thrive. That's the circle of life…or a garden's life!

Marilyn Pabon

What About Protein?

In a crisis meat may be unavailable, scarce or at the very least, expensive, but if you have a food garden in your yard you will be assured you will have food to eat and the ability to feed your family. The most asked question is "Can you be healthy on fruits and vegetables without meat for protein?"

Humans are able to survive as herbivores and carnivores and omnivores. However, surviving and thriving are two different things. Optimal health and nutrition for humans comes from plant food. Our anatomy and physiology is much more in line with that of an herbivorous diet. Our bodies are made to process the difficult-to-digest plant food with the way we chew, our teeth shape, create saliva, swallow, store food in our stomach (or lack of storage), ferment food, digest food, and absorb nutrients. It is truly amazing what our bodies can do when they are given the proper fuel to get us not only through the day but to make it easier for us to truly thrive.

We thrive on plant food but when it is scarce or unavailable we can survive on meat until plant food is available again, as was the case for the ancients. Meat is a survival food to keep us alive in times of winter and famine but becomes unhealthful when eaten in excess year round.

Meats, of all kinds, are unnatural food. Flesh, fowl and sea foods are very likely to contain numbers of bacteria that infect the intestines, causing colitis and many other diseases. They always cause putrefaction.

It is an established fact that meat protein causes putrefaction twice as quickly as vegetable protein. There is no ingredient in meat, except B12, that cannot be procured in products of the vegetable kingdom. Meat is an expensive second-hand food material and will not make healthy, pure blood or form good tissues. The nutritive value of meat broths is practically nothing. They always contain uric acid and other poisons.

B12 vitamin is needed in the smallest amount, only three millionths of a gram per day. Miso and comfrey are sources of B12 as are fortified plant milks, cereals and B12 supplements.

As our population increases there seems to be an endless need for more water for industry, agriculture, drinking and other uses, more and more of the water supply is becoming contaminated and unfit for use. How is this connected to meat eating? 2,500 gallons of water a day are required to provide food for the meat eater, but only 300 gallons a day are needed for the vegetarian.

Another perspective is to realize that 21 pounds of protein must be fed to cattle in order to get 1 pound of protein in return. The difference between the amount of protein fed to cattle and the amount returned is enough to meet 90 percent of the world's protein deficiency if it were fed to them as cereal.

The argument that flesh must be eaten in order to supply the body with sufficient protein is unreasonable. Protein is found in beans, peas, lentils, nuts of all kinds, and soy beans. There are many reasons why some people choose not to eat meat. Among these are religious, ethical, economic, and ecological reasons; but the main reason is to have better health.

Our Creator made humans from the dust of the earth. The different properties that are found in the earth are found in humans, fruits, grains, nuts and vegetables; all contain the same elements which are in the soil. When these fruits, vegetables, nuts and grains are eaten in their natural state, instead of being robbed of their life-giving properties during preparation, human health, beauty and happiness will be the reward. Herbs, flowers, leaves, roots and the bark of trees are the medicine from Mother Nature. The fundamental principle of true healing consists of a return to natural living habits.

The Bottom Line

If you find yourself in a crisis or disaster and food or money is in short supply do not fret or worry about not having meat to eat. It is not a necessary food unless there is nothing else to eat.

Whether you cut out or cut down on meat you will be healthier for it. Deciding now to adopt a plant based diet not only will make you healthier to live through a possible food crises and it will also be much easier for you to adjust to processed food shortages. Learning how to grow fresh food now just may save your life in the future. In the meantime living a whole food, plant based lifestyle that prevents disease, supports wellness and longevity and nourishes the mind, body and spirit will prepare you for whatever may come our way.

You don't have to be a master gardener to have a successful victory garden, although it doesn't hurt to get tips from someone who is. With a little bit of planning and preparation, you can have a beautiful garden that provides you with colorful, nutritious food at a fraction of the cost of the grocery store.

Who knows what other global events are waiting in the future. If you plant a garden now, you'll be better prepared to provide for yourself and your family no matter what happens. Best of all, you can control exactly what you grow and the methods you use. There's nothing better than fresh vegetables straight from your own garden, ripe fruit picked off your own trees and bushes and delicious herbs to add flavor and minerals to your dishes!

CHAPTER 7

Grow Your Own Food

*"The glory of gardening: hands in the
dirt, head in the sun, heart with nature.
To nurture a garden is to feed not just
the body, but the soul."* Alfred Austin

In ancient times, humans were keenly attuned to the heartbeat
of the planet. Life was lived on the edge. Their survival as a
species depended on their ability to live in harmony with the
world. Reverence and interconnection were the foundation of
their relationship with nature.

Our ancestors believed the earth has a living spirit. They
called her Mother because she nourished them and gave them
everything they needed to live. Many indigenous communities
have always practiced a regenerative, stewardship relationship to
the planet. They were children of the Earth.

Being in nature can restore our mood, give us back our energy
and vitality, refresh and rejuvenate us. Human beings were meant
to be nourished and fed by nature. Our mind, body and soul
needs it. When we work the earth with our hands we are truly
reconnecting with Mother Nature as it is meant to be.

As the physical embodiment of the Divine Feminine, Mother Earth is our ultimate provider. She sustains us, protects us, and allows us to flourish. We are birthed within her, and we will die within her. And each and every day, she has endless reminders to share with us that reflect the divinity, joy, beauty, and love inherent in life.

Growing your own food is as natural as breathing. There are so many different reasons to start your garden. Whether you want a garden filled with beauty, to grow your own food for better health, or create an outdoor living space you can survive on, gardening is good for the soul. Most encouraging is the message that home gardens will help reconnect us to ourselves, one another, and nature in a way that all of us can relate to on the most personal level: growing and consuming some to most of our own food.

With all the uncertainty of our current times including the industrial food system, having food security close by is a comfort. Growing food with and for the ones you love has a magical way of bringing people together and making everyone healthier in the process.

It's What You Know That Will Save You

I once heard that when an emergency happens, it's not what you have that's most important, it's what you know. While some people have gotten comfort from stockpiling toilet paper, I've found great comfort in my gardening, preserving, herbalism, and holistic health knowledge. Even the most robust stockpile runs out, but my ability to grow my own food and medicine never will.

If your garden becomes a significant source of food for your family, it is vital that you are growing foods in organically cultivated ground, without the use of industrial chemical fertilizer, which will meet many of your nutritional needs. Deficiency of vitamins and elements in food is the result of the destruction of the soil by tilling and adding chemical fertilizers, herbicides, pesticides and GMO seeds.

Organic gardening includes the rebuilding of the soil through the live processes of soil organisms such as earthworms and bacteria. Only in this manner adopted by Mother Nature, since vegetation began on the face of the earth, can we produce a fertile and productive ground on which to grow food with an abundance of vitamins and minerals. Fruits and vegetables grown in such soil need no poison, dusting or spraying. Insects and pests do not destroy crops as the birds in the natural course of events feed on them. This "new, old approach" to gardening and farming is called "regenerative agriculture" that has the potential to balance our climate, replenish our vast water supplies, and feed the world.

If your area has short growing seasons, growing foods which store well is essential. Regardless of family favorites, there are some foods which are necessities in a survival garden. Grow all the food that you feasibly can on your own property. Berry bushes, grapevines, fruit trees, plant them if your climate is right for their growth. Grow vegetables and eat them from your own yard. Make your gardens neat and attractive as well as productive.

Having the knowledge to maintain a garden that will provide for you and your family could one day become vital to your survival. Most people will know the basics of gardening but maintaining a garden that provides for your family requires some special knowledge. Home and community gardens allow the food insecure to grow their own food, instead of relying on temporary handouts from food banks, should it ever come to that.

You can build a survival vegetable garden in small areas and if you are a beginner gardener it is best to start small. Even if you only have a balcony or windowsill, you can still have a productive beautiful garden. If you have some sort of outdoor space that is exposed to the sun for at least 4-6 hours per day, you can grow some of your own food.

If you have a balcony available: Collect as many large

containers as you can find. These don't have to be traditional pots, they can be whiskey barrels, five gallon buckets, and even small trash cans work. Just make sure you poke or drill holes in the bottom of repurposed containers for drainage. Also, don't forget that you can grow in hanging baskets that hang on the balcony railing.

If you have a small amount of green space available: A single 8'x4' raised bed or even a square 4'x4' bed can produce an absolute TON of food. If you have a patio or a small yard, a raised bed is the way to go.

There are plans for raised beds, short and tall, that are convenient and look nice but they can be pricey to build and probably not the right option if you are wanting to build a quick survival garden. If you want to do it affordably and quickly, you can use half cinder blocks to form the outside of your bed. Half cinder blocks (4" cinder blocks) run around $1.50 each, and you can build a very sturdy 8'x4' bed with them for less than $30. It takes less than 20 minutes to form the bed, and you can also grow herbs and flowers in the holes of the cinder block to utilize every space you have.

What you can and should grow will depend highly on your available space.

- Fruits
- vegetables
- herbs
- teas
- flowers

Gardening - Growing Your Own Food

Backyard gardening, while it is starting to make a comeback, is still not very common. Many people don't do it because they believe that in order to grow food, you have to have a lot of land. Nothing could be further from the truth!

You can grow food on your balcony if you live in an apartment. You would be surprised how many tomatoes you get off of just one plant. Same with peppers. You don't need to live on acres of land to have a food garden. Some plants will even grow inside, on your window sill. Vertical gardening and Square Foot Gardening is also gaining popularity, as is hydroponics, which is growing plants in water instead of soil.

We do not need pretty grass, seriously. Tear out decorative shrubs and put some blueberry bushes in their place. Grow a few fruit trees. Make a raised bed garden. Just go with the mentality of growing food instead of lawns. Edible lawns can even be pretty! It amazes me how beautiful some edibles really are when they grow. Well-manicured lawns became important landscaping in the 50's and 60's suburbia, it's time to get over it and move on with more sensible designs.

Community gardens are becoming more popular each year. They are popping up more frequently in urban, and even suburban areas. This is great. Even if you don't have room because you live in an apartment, or have a small lot, or covenants that do not allow you to garden. You can start up or join, a community garden. It can be a lot of fun and they benefit lots of people.

Growing your own food is a win/win situation on many levels:

- Saves money
- Pesticide Free
- Healthier (no chemical fertilizer)
- Convenient (you don't have to go to the store)
- Sets a good example to kids, friends and neighbors to be more self-reliant

If you have never had a garden, now is a good time to start.

If you feel daunted, then try container gardening first and then move on to ground gardening, if you have the space.

The truth about long term survival in hard times is that you are far more likely to die from starvation than from a bullet. If you are concerned about what the future may bring, but otherwise in a good place, now is the time to prepare and learn survival skills such as growing your own food to stay alive and healthy.

Save Seeds From What You Are Eating

While we should do this even in good times, it's imperative in times of a food shortage to use everything you have. Seeds are being taken over by big business, they are being altered, genetically modified, and becoming expensive to purchase.

What fresh produce are you eating now? Make sure it is organic so the seeds you save will grow properly. Perhaps you can plant a potato, start slips on a sweet potato, and dry out seeds from tomatoes, peppers, and peas.

Research online how to dry out and plant seeds from fruits and vegetables you are currently eating.

How To Plan A Survival Garden

First of all, with any small garden, I recommend utilizing the Square Foot Gardening method, which is basically just a method of planning your garden space by dividing it into square feet, and then planting certain numbers of crops in each square. Using this method of planning allows you to get the highest production per inch in your small garden. There is a ton of information about this method online.

Killing the Grass and Weeds

Before you plant anything you need to kill the grass and weeds in your garden space, without using chemical poisons. I have found that laying black plastic over the garden area for a few weeks and letting the suns heat kill everything underneath works well if I am not in a hurry to get the garden planted. You can also place layers of newspaper or cardboard over the garden space and shovel a thick layer of garden soil on top of it, then add another layer of mulch. When using cardboard or newspapers, several layers will be necessary. The sheeting layer will kill any grass or weeds below it, turning it into compost to feed the soil. This process can take a long time to yield results, so it's best to prepare the garden in the fall. That way, the garden will be ready to be planted in the spring.

No-Till Gardening

For healthy soil continue to add mulch, leaves, bark chips and compost throughout the year. I like using the no-till method of gardening, also called Back to Eden, no dig, deep mulch system, lasagna gardening and regenerative gardening. A no-till garden is a method of gardening that does away with the traditional use of tilling to prepare the soil. Tilling reduces the moisture content of the soil and disturbs the living microorganisms living in the soil, which is a process that is accelerates erosion. It also harms earthworms and microorganisms that enrich the soil by adding nitrogen and turning the earth. Tilling destroys the root structure of the previous year's crops, which can actually enhance the nutrient base of soil if they are left to decompose naturally.

In no-till gardens, the soil is not dug up, instead organic components are layered over the soil to create a rich, nutrient-heavy base much like the natural rich layers of the forest floor. Over the space of a few seasons, the fertility of your soil will improve dramatically, and it will actually become easier to prepare your garden for planting.

Putting together a no-till garden is really very easy to do and requires far less time and effort than that of tilling. It takes a bit of time to prepare a garden for planting, but the end result will be a healthy soil base and a bountiful harvest.

Choose a Planting Space

Before beginning, decide where to plant a vegetable garden and the garden size. It is imperative to pick a sunny spot, preferably south-facing, to take maximum advantage of the sunlight shed on the garden.

It is not necessary to have a large plot because plants can be rotated and gardeners can facilitate several plantings each season. For gardeners who are short on space, consider starting a raised bed or a container garden. Either style of garden requires very little room, and the concepts of no-till, compost layering gardening can be applied to both.

Plan Out Garden Beds

When the materials needed are ready, start thinking about what to plant and the spacing of garden beds. The key to successful no-till gardening is not to disturb the soil structure by walking on it. It's important to layout beds with walkways and stepping stones between them so that no one is stepping on and tamping down the soil.

Raised bed and container gardens make it easier to work without disturbing the soil surrounding the plants. Whichever method is chosen, even if it's traditional in-ground beds, just make sure plenty of space is accessible between the beds to move around. It is best to restrict the size of each bed to a maximum of 4 feet wide by 8 feet long so all plants can be easily reached.

Prepare the Soil

Add compost! This is perhaps the most expensive part of no-till gardening, especially when trying to create a very large garden. Create compost from kitchen and garden scraps, buy it by the bag, or purchase it in bulk from a nursery supply store. If preparing the garden in the fall, you can also add manure with or in place of the compost.

The cardboard and newspaper will pretty much decompose into the soil, if some of this type of sheeting is still intact, leave it in place and simply layer compost over it.

Spread a thick, even layer of compost over the soil in the garden beds, at least 2 inches thick. Do not turn the soil beforehand or dig in the compost. Add in chicken fertilizer and other organic materials like grass clippings at this point. Also, add a layer of mulch (wood chips, straw, hay, grass clippings, shredded leaves, etc) over the compost to discourage weed growth and to encourage moisture retention.

Put in Seeds or Starters

Once a compost layer has been put in, then immediately start to plant the garden. Plant either from seed or starter seedlings from a nursery. Gently hollow away the mulch and compost layer to make room for starters by using hands. Seeds can just be pressed into the soil with fingers and covered in a light layer of enriched compost soil.

It is not necessary to dig into the soil to plant seedlings. That would disturb and break up the soil below, leaving an unhealthy substrate.

Maintenance

Maintaining a no-till garden is really not that different from maintaining a traditional garden. It is necessary to weed around plants once every few days, there will always be a few stubborn weeds and grasses that will persistently try to come up. It's one of the unavoidable realities of gardening, whichever method is used.

Gardeners usually find that it is not necessary to water the garden as heavily because the mulch and compost layers over the soil act to trap in moisture. Less fertilizing is also required because the thick compost layer will contain most of the fertilizer the plants need. This also mitigates the possibility of root damage from using chemical fertilizers, pesticides, herbicides and fungicides, which all kill living soil.

Harvesting and Bedding Down

Once the final harvest of the season comes around, gardeners start bedding down the garden in preparation for winter and the next spring. Cut back any remaining plants to just above the soil level.

The residual stumps and root systems will act as additional organic matter to enrich the soil. Spread a thick layer of mulch over the soil, the mulch will break down over the winter. Use whatever kind of organic material that can be found for free!

The following spring, all gardeners will need to do is add another layer of compost and mulch. This will allow the soil to keep building up its nutrient base, making it fertile and allowing it to retain moisture. Although planting from seed is possible, it's easier for seedlings to thrive in a no-till garden because they are not competing with older root structures for space and nutrients.

No-till gardening might seem labor-intensive at the start, but it actually needs far less effort than traditional gardening systems that require tilling or deep digging to prepare the ground. Once the garden is prepared for the first season, the subsequent growing seasons will require less and less preparation. All that will be necessary is add a couple of inches of compost to garden beds each year.

Notes:

- Vegetable gardens need an inch of water per week, with container gardens needing slightly more. If the soil feels dry, your garden needs water. It's better to water a little bit every day as opposed to watering once per week, especially if it's hot out.
- Mulch is your friend. Once your plants are established, put a thick layer of mulch around each plant to keep weeds down and keep moisture in. Mulch options: straw, pine shavings, wood chips, seedless grass clippings, newspaper.
- Weeds are your foe. Weeds compete with your garden plants for nutrients and water, so keep your beds weed-free. This should be relatively easy since we're talking about small beds here. Weeding by hand is a good exercise in mindfulness.
- Most plants WANT to be picked. Clipping herbs, harvesting beans, picking cucumbers; it signals to the plant to produce more fruit. Leaving ripe vegetables on the vine signals to the plant that the season is over and the plant goes dormant, starts to seed, or just dies.
- Visit your garden every single day. Not only is it a good opportunity to check in and check soil moisture, pick

goodies, and weed, but it also is good for your mental health.

- Compost is the only fertilizer you really need in an emergency. If you have a good compost handy, you can use it to top dress (sprinkle around the base of the plant) if a plant is looking a little sick.
- Save your seeds for next seasons crop and be sure to have your favorite seeds in your emergency food storage.
- Companion planting is one of the most beneficial ways to grow a garden. Growing certain plants together can encourage healthy growth, repel harmful insects, and attract beneficial insects. Flowers can be planted in your vegetable garden to achieve a healthier and thriving garden.
- Edible landscaping: You may not have the space or need for a traditional vegetable garden but you can certainly plant herbs and vegetables throughout your existing landscaping to be more self-reliant.
- Plant flowers to attract bees, butterflies and hummingbirds to pollinate your fruit and vegetable gardens. Without the bees and pollination your flowers wont develop into fruits, nuts and veggies.
- You can make plans. But the garden retains its capacity to surprise, sometimes dashing your hopes and dreams, other times dependably delivering rewards. The garden is a fantastic teacher.

I hope this has inspired and empowered you to be more self-reliant and grow your own food at home, there has never been a better time to start than now, before you are in an emergency situation. It is very satisfying to know you have fresh food to eat in your backyard and you don't have to eat food which has had to travel hundreds of miles to get to you, and has been picked too early and been touched my many hands before you pick it up and bring it home. Join the home grown food movement. Happy growing!

On A Larger Scale

Besides your personal self-reliance on growing your own food you may be interested in the bigger picture of healing the farming soil which will produce more organic food and in turn reduce carbon in the atmosphere which could potentially reverse global warming.

There are grassroots movements which are trying to educate farmers in the no till/plowing farming method which could heal the land and the planet. It is an uphill battle to educate farmers on the importance of the health of soil and what that means. They also have to be willing to forgo government welfare subsidies which oblige them to grow what and how they are told.

Regenerative Agriculture is a system of farming principles and practices that increases biodiversity, enriches soils, improves watersheds, and enhances ecosystem services. It aims to capture carbon in the soil and above ground biomass (plants), reversing current global trends of atmospheric accumulation and climate change. At the same time, it offers increased yields, resilience to climate instability, and higher health and vitality for farming and ranching communities.

It's important to avoid plowing the soil, and abstain from using harmful chemical amendments. These practices make it difficult for a complex soil ecosystem to thrive. Keeping the soil covered with living plants or trampled/dead plant material reduces erosion and helps lower soil temperatures.

Keeping living roots in the ground year-round (or for as long as possible) provides a steady source of food for organisms in the soil. In turn, soil microorganisms help prevent soil erosion, increase water infiltration rates, and provide plants with key nutrients.

Growing a diversity of plants helps cultivate nutrient dense soil, increase soil carbon, and reduce the risk of pests and diseases.

Including animals in farming systems closes the nutrient loop and reduces the need for imported fertilizers. Deciding which are the right species of animals to incorporate depends on each farm's unique ecosystem and climate.

No two farms are alike. From brittle environments to more moist ones, from different crops to livestock, from no funds to extensive funds, context is key. How you will go about regenerating land will vary and depend on many key components. A holistic framework is necessary to successfully transition to regenerative.

Purchasing from farmers that are building healthy soil is good for both you and the climate. Regenerative agricultural systems produce healthier and tastier food, support clean air and water, and contribute a better world to future generations.

Being self-sufficient isn't just for homesteaders. Anyone can benefit from having a variety of fresh vegetables and herbs in their yard. Not only do you reduce your carbon footprint by reducing how much you rely on commercially-produced food, but you also get the advantages of truly fresh vegetables. As soon as food is harvested, it begins to lose moisture and nutrients. By the time it's transported from a farm to the grocery store in your area, it has lost considerable health value. However, when you grow your own food, you can eat it fresh from the garden, which means you get all the flavor and nutrition available.

When you grow food yourself, you can control exactly how it's treated from start to finish. Everything from the type of fertilizer you use, to whether you grow organically is in your hands. You don't have to guess how a farmer chose to operate, and you can skip the harmful chemicals in most grocery-store produce.

A variety of studies have shown the link between the availability of fresh food and the overall health of a community. When you garden and encourage those around you to do so as well, you're helping prevent food deserts and promoting better mental and physical health for everyone involved. A garden at your home allows you to take care of yourself even when supply chains are interrupted. Even better, many plants produce an abundance of crops, which will enable you to share and care for others as well.

Where to Begin

If this speaks to you and lights you up, a good place to learn more about how we can participate in improving our food, repairing the earth's soil, and reverse global warming before it destroys the world; watch this documentary called "Kiss The Ground", website: kisstheground.com.

CHAPTER 8

Bees

*"Be warned: if you start keeping bees
and develop a real interest in them, it will
be with you for life. And I doubt very much
that you will regret it for a moment."*

**Philip Chandler, author of
The Barefoot Beekeeper**

Humans have always had a close relationship with bees. Honey
has probably been a staple food for humans for as long as there
have been humans. Beekeeping is one of the earliest skills of
settled farm based society and culture. Bees, and other insects,
made settled farming possible through their action of pollination
of fruit trees, especially apple trees, and other food crops.

Bees not only provide food through honey and their gathered
pollens, but their waxes have been essential for effective medicines
and as an aid in metalworking. Beeswax was an essential ingredient
in the creation of effigies used in rituals, so crafting with beeswax
was an important trade to learn.

- Honey was the only sweetener of the ancient world and its maker, the honey bee, is both industrious and magical.
- Only the female bees build hives and make honey, and they communicate with each other via dance-language.
- Honey is the only food that will not rot. A jar of honey may remain edible for over 3,000 years.
- Women were the first beekeepers, the honey bee has always symbolized matriarchy.

Bees have been sacred to the Divine Feminine for thousands of years in ancient civilizations from Babylon to Rome. Virtually all bees, except the drones, are female and they serve a single Queen Bee. Only bees can perform the transformative magic of turning pollen into honey. In ancient times, honey was the only sweetener available. It was also a powerful and much valued preservative. Honey was accordingly seen as one of the most precious gifts of the Goddess.

The bee was always a sign of the Goddess. Time and again we see priestesses and goddesses of the ancient world referred to as bee priestesses and bee goddesses. Many goddesses of old have their names and titles in someway mythologically or etymologically connected to the words for bees and or honey.

For tens of thousands of years humans have plundered the hives of wild bees for their precious honey and beeswax. 9,000 years ago humans started keeping bees in pottery vessels in North Africa. 4,500 years ago bees were domesticated in Egypt. On the walls of the sun temple of Nyuserre Ini from the Fifth Dynasty, before 2422 BCE, workers are depicted blowing smoke into hives as they are removing honeycombs.

The Sumarian medicine men from the Mesopotamian civilization of Sumer, who flourished between 5300 - 3500 BC, are told as being the originators of apitherapy, caring and healing with products from the bees.

The bee and its products had an importance that was not only agricultural, but also nutritional, medicinal and ritualistic. Honey was more than just food, it was applied to wounds for its antiseptic properties and was believed to prevent miscarriages. Beeswax was used in mummification and in candle making.

The Sumerians also appear to have been the first to depict winged figures in art, including humans with wings, including images of the Bee Goddess. Could the Bee Goddess have been the inspiration and archetype for biblical angels?

Beekeeping continues to this day, where we now have developed hives that allow us to harvest honey without destroying the entire colony. But bees are in decline. Since 2006 colony losses from Colony Collapse Disorder have been increasing across the world although the causes of the syndrome are, as yet, unknown. It could be all the pesticides and poison that mankind is releasing into nature, or it could be something else, either way the bees are dying at a disturbing rate. But we need them for our very survival because of their role in pollinating our crops.

The Dance of the Bee Goddess

- Bees are the only insect that communicates through dance. When bees find a new food source, that is too far away to be smelled or seen, they go back to the hive and dance.
- Their dance tells the other bees both the direction and how far away the food source is. The dance is complex and seemingly too inspired to be a life feature that evolved.
- The scout bee dances on the honeycomb in the hive. The other bees then follow the dancer and imitate her movements precisely.
- The bees also take in and memorize the fragrance of the pollen in the nectar.

- If the food source is within about 50 meters of the hive, the scout bee does a circular dance on the honeycomb. If the food source is further away the scout bee does a figure of eight dance, known as a "waggle dance". The direction and angle the dancing bee cuts across the diameter of the circle also reveals the direction of the food.

Current Bee Crisis

The serious decline in bee health around the world, especially in the USA where the wild bees are almost extinct and in Europe that is catching up to the USA, is revealing how our ways are endangering the balance of all living things. Bees represent the biggest disaster that is happening on our planet, and it can be reversed with collective effort.

Ancient legends have foretold that if the bees died and became extinct in this world, human extinction would soon follow. Albert Einstein predicted if the bees went extinct, humans would only be four years behind them. The current bee crisis is a global crisis. Without the pollination of blossoms by bees, we will no longer have fruits, nuts, and many kinds of vegetables.

It has been my personal experience that every year for the last five consecutive years we have had fewer and fewer bees in our yard and gardens, to the point of needing to hand pollinate squash and melon flowers. Without pollination the flowers whither and die without setting their fruit.

The Many Different Types Of Bees

There are many different types of bees that all work to help ensure that our native flowers, plants, trees, fruits, and vegetables are pollinated, and that biodiversity is maintained. While some we may be more familiar with than others, all bees have their role in helping to maintain biodiversity on this planet.

Honeybees:

Honeybees, like the name suggests, are famous for making honey and are a colonizing bee that is excellent for farming as they are easy to contain and move from farm-to-farm for pollination. Honeybees, however, are not native to North America and were brought to North America during colonial times for their honey and wax producing capabilities that made them highly valuable.

But while honeybees may be high on peoples priority list for protection (as they should be) there are more than 4,000 other native bee species living in North America alone that are primarily responsible for pollinating our native plants and have been the silent backbone for maintaining biodiversity.

Native Bees:

The most well-known native bee in North America is the bumblebee, which is also the only social native bee that lives in colonies (similar to honeybees) and has a fuzzy coat that makes it capable of withstanding colder climates. All other native bees prefer to be solitary and will live on their own with 75% actually making their homes underground.

Other kinds of native bees include:

Mason bees: These bees love berry plants and fruit trees and will live in hollow wood or stems.

Leafcutter bees: Will cut small round holes in plant leaves and in return pollinate your garden. These bees love native flowers, melons, milkweed and alfalfa.

Sweet Bees: Sweet bees are ground-nesting, meaning that they make their homes underground and are great for your garden as they love pollinating vegetables and wild flowers.

Carpenter Bees: These bees are large and one of the most common types of bees in North America. They love pollinating vegetables and wild flowers, which makes them a great friend for your home garden.

Mining Bees: Mining bees love wild flowers and native perennials. These bees will dig into the ground and into lawns, which is another reason why keeping your lawn free of pesticides is so important.

Learning to identify and appreciate the pollinators in your garden adds another dimension to your life with bees. When you recognize wild species and understand how they compare and contrast with honey bees, you become a better, more nuanced beekeeper. So take a closer look and discover who is really pollinating your garden.

Enjoy watching bees gather nectar from flowers but give them space. I know it is almost impossible to do but try to resist swinging your arms and swatting when a bee flies close by. Threatened bees are attracted to movement. Swatting will not encourage the bees to settle down. Move away. And don't go outside smelling like a flower garden, bees are very sensitive to scent and may seek you out.

Things You Can Do To Help Your Local Bees

Bees are often feared by kids and adults given their ability to sting, but what we really should be fearing isn't the bee, but life without them. With 1/3 of our global food supply relying on pollinators like bees, as well as many of our favorite herbs and flowers, a world without bees would result in a food security emergency and a much less beautiful planet. So rather than fearing bees we should be celebrating and protecting them, and teaching our children to do the same.

There are so many ways you can help save the bees within your own yard, community, and state. In fact, I would argue that starting at home and then expanding your advocacy locally is the best place to start. Every single movement has local roots attached to it and is powered by motivated, passionate individuals. Which is why often the best place to begin advocating for change is close by within your own home and local community.

- Plant bee friendly native flowers and herbs
- Bees are attracted to violet/blue colored flowers; borage, cornflower, rosemary, bluebells, verbena, bergamot, echinacea, hebe, snapdragons
- Don't use chemicals in your garden or on your lawn
- Put a small basin of fresh water outside
- Buy local raw honey
- Buy local organic food
- Advocate for bee protection at local, state and federal level
- Attend town hall meetings and bring town policies like banning glyphosate and neonicotinoids from being used in your town.
- Propose community garden projects that encourage the planting of native, bee-friendly plants.
- Email your congressional representatives and senators to advocate policies in favor of saving the bees.
- Educate your friends and family about how they can protect bees

Provide a Bee Friendly Garden

To make a bee friendly garden, avoid using harmful pesticides and fertilizers in your garden. Go Organic! Bees are so tender that chemicals in these products directly influence their life.

Grow more local and native plants in your garden because the native bees attract towards more native and wild varieties of plants than exotic and fancy ones. Of course there are always those non native plants like butterfly bush and firecracker that attract them. You'll also need to grow less hybrid flowers; hybridized flowers are showy and hardy but contain less or no pollen.

Single petaled flowers have only one ring of petals and they provide more nectar and pollen than double petaled flowers. Also, pollinators prefer specific designs, sizes, smell and colors of flowers. For an example, bees love to feed on small flowers and hummingbirds draw towards large flowers.

Plan for year round blooming of flowers to attract bees in your garden, choose annuals and perennials equally. Plant flowers that bloom season by season: crocus, borage, calendula and lilacs for spring. Bee balm, cosmos, marigold, sunflower, petunias and snapdragons for summer; zinnias, aster and gaillardia for fall.

Bees flicker from flower to flower that's why growing flowers in clusters is a good idea. You can do companion planting for this. Always prefer bright and cool colored flowers like blue, yellow, white. Bees avoid dark and bold colored flowers.

In colder climates, many bee species stop buzzing in winters, bumblebees go to hibernation, solitary bees die off and others migrate to more temperate parts. Still, there are a few bee species like common carder and black bee that are hardy to cold climate, but die off due to lack of flowers. Take special care in winter, if you're living in a colder zone; grow more winter flowers like narcissus, cowslip, ground ivy etc.

Not only flowers, these pollinators attract towards fruits, veggies and herbs, too. In herbs, grow catmint, lemon balm, oregano and cilantro. Grow fruits like peach, blackberry, guava, strawberries and passion fruits, they're full of nectar. In vegetables, grow squashes, gourds and peppers.

Don't pull weeds like milkweed, dandelion, lantana and clover; they are really important to pollinators like bees and butterflies that feed on them. If you fear weeds will invade your garden, then grow them in large containers and do deadheading to avoid seedpods from forming.

Bees drink water too, more in spring and summer from shallow water sources like puddles, dog bowls, and small ponds and creeks. You must arrange a water source for them. If you have a water pond already, you don't need to do anything, otherwise install a dripping faucet and place a wooden board under it. Water will drip and not only bees, butterflies will drink from it, too. You can also put a plate or bowl of water near the flowering plants.

Replacing your lawn will not only save you from its maintenance, water and a lot of money but if you can't sacrifice your lawn, at least cut down its area, grow flowers around the outer edges. You can also grow herbs like rosemary, thyme, basil, borage and lavender.

Many homeowners today want more of a natural look and feel, even letting some wild flowers and flowering weeds flourish in their lawn, and allowing their green space to have a more complete ecosystem. Still others object to how much of suburbia is grass. Imagine if people planted Victory Gardens (vegetable gardens) instead!

As we become illuminated to the consequences of how we live, how we consume and dispose, and what we put our faith in, which has been damaging our planet's health, we need to re-connect to natural ways to live with nurture and sustain our Mother Earth.

To truly honor Mother Earth is to respect her through our actions. By committing to a sustainable, low-waste, and ethical way of living, we are putting our head where our heart is.

The magic our ancestors found in bees and their hive life seems to be entering our psyche again. It's my hope that some of you Divine Feminine goddesses reading this book will get started with beekeeping. The world needs more beekeepers. Why not you?

CHAPTER 9

Flower Gardens

*"Don't wear perfume in the garden, unless
you want to be pollinated by bees." ~ Anne Raver*

Flowers carry a very pure and uplifting vibration of peace, harmony and joy. Flowers are a clear expression of the divine within nature. The divine feminine craves to create and embody beauty, internal and external. That includes not only the soul and body, but also the places we live.

Flowers and plants all possess a unique vibrational energy. With their simple elegance, vibrant colors and natural, grounding energy, flowers have a mystical way of raising our spirits and raising the vibrational energy of our bodies. Subconsciously, we are often drawn toward the flowers that most closely match our current state of being.

All flowers carry healing and uplifting vibrations which will help you on your spiritual path. For countless centuries, the aroma of flowers has been used in perfumes and cosmetics to enhance the allure and the expression of femininity.

Each flower has a unique color and vibrational frequency that resonates with one, or more, of the seven chakras in our body. Flowers also help us balance our divine feminine energies.

"Stop and smell the roses" may have a deeper meaning than you realize. Roses carry the high vibration of love and passion. Traditionally known as a "flower of love" roses will indeed attract love into your experience.; romantic love, self- love and unconditional love.

A bouquet of flowers can transform a space or brighten someone's day. Flowers bring joy for those who receive them, but also to those who grow them. Don't wait for someone to give you flowers, plant your own flower garden.

Whether gardening for survival, as a hobby or for landscaping purposes, toiling in the flowers and dirt allows you to work through your thoughts and emotions. Gardening allows you to be angry, disappointed, happy, sad, or confused, all while not feeling judged. The plants and flowers welcome you back no matter what state you were in the day before.

As spring wears off and summer heat picks up, most gardeners find it rather tiring to work in the garden. That's why you need to look for flowering plants, both annuals and perennials, that bloom profusely throughout the seasons without much pampering from you.

There are many flower options to choose from:

- annual
- perennial
- edible flowers
- cutting flowers
- wild flowers
- flowers for drying
- moon gardens
- hanging gardens
- gardens for butterflies, bees, humming birds
- gardens for flagrance

- self seeding flowers
- flowering trees and bushes
- medicinal garden
- tea garden
- herb gardens

Light Up Your Garden

Whether you're hosting a garden party or want to dine al fresco with loved ones, a touch of light is a must-have for when the summer evenings start to draw in. Alternatively, they create excellent mood lighting, they show off your white and light color flowers, perfect for having a romantic night under the moon and stars or for relaxing in peace on your own.

Bring The Flowers Inside

Flower planting, harvesting, and arranging can be a very enjoyable activity. Even the darkest of spirits brighten at the sight of a well-arranged bouquet of flowers.

Composing Your Flower Arrangements: You need to remember three things when putting together your flower arrangements; thriller, filler and spiller.

The thriller is your "money flower". These flowers are usually a little larger, pop out of an arrangement, and more expensive per stem, but add "pop" and serious value to your arrangement.

The fillers make up the structure of the arrangement. These are often branching stems that add volume and architecture to the bouquet. You should vary the sizes of your fillers to create interest.

The spillers are the flowers with gentle or dramatic curves that spill over the edge of the vase to give the arrangement length and keep it from looking too top-heavy.

Those skilled at flower arranging can create a masterpiece with ten different varieties of flowers. If you're new to flower arranging, however, stick to three to five varieties to keep the arrangement interesting, but not chaotic. Also choose a color theme for your arrangement. For example, you could choose two different shades of orange, and a purple to accent.

Self Reliance:

You may be asking "What do flowers have to do with self-reliance?"

Growing your own flowers has many personal benefits:

- It promotes physical exercise and being out in the fresh air gives a sense of well-being like getting back to nature.
- Due to the sedentary nature of many jobs and hobbies, the amount of physical activity that people get weekly is way below the amount recommended by the Center for Disease Control. Adults should exercise at least 2 hours and 30 minute a week. Children should have at least 1 hour a day of physical activity. Planting, weeding and watering plants all require some degree of daily physical activity. Keeping to a weekly workout regime prolongs life by fighting disease and strengthening muscles and bones. Gardening will allow people to achieve most of their weekly physical activity quota.
- A side effect of today's sedentary lifestyle is the unnaturally pale skin and a disturbingly low amount of Vitamin D in the body. Vitamin D enters the body when ultraviolet radiation touches the skin. Without the Vitamin D that is produced when you engage in outside activities like gardening, you will have weak bones and teeth and disturbingly high dentist and doctor's bills.

- This may seem obvious but flowers are beautiful and they can bring you and all who see them joy. Planting flowers will make your yard beautiful for the whole neighborhood to enjoy and give you a sense of accomplishment being a co-creator with Mother Nature.

- A Divine Feminine doesn't sit around and wait for a man to bring her flowers. She plants a flower garden and surrounds herself with the beauty, flagrance and high vibrational energy her flowers bring to her.

- There is enjoyment when flowers are harvested and arranged in a vase to view daily as you practice extreme feminine self-care.

- Your own organically grown cut flowers helps the mind and the body stay active and lifts the spirit.

- Flowers are also hugely beneficial for bees & insects providing food & habitats for them and the bees & insects in turn help to pollinate your other flowers & veggies. Flower growing helps to maintain a healthier eco-system.

- By planting flowers, people can lower their carbon foot print by supplying the environment with more plants that can consume more carbon dioxide. Through photosynthesis the oxygen supply is then replenished a bit.

- Growing flowers also allows you to appreciate the seasons and be in tune with what flowers when and for how long.

- Flowers make your garden look beautiful and create a peaceful and relaxing environment, your own little piece of heaven on earth, your contribution to beautify the world around you.

Divine Feminine Flower Fragrances

Flowers are a physical representation of the Divine Feminine. They are the offspring born of Mother Earth, the symbol of perfect femininity. They aid in the restoration of proper order and balance with the Divine Feminine. When we are in the midst of our flower gardens we are in the presence of truth and beauty, both of which represent the principles of the Divine Feminine.

Aromatherapy isn't a new age phenomenon. People have been using aromatic plants, flowers, herbs and oils for longer than recorded history.

Rose

The rose is considered to be the flower of the goddess in general. It was even assigned to the Divine Mother Mary. The aroma and image of pink roses persists in visions of the faithful, despite having been replaced by the more modest white lily by a medieval church council.

The personality type that personifies rose is sensual but also comforting. It is exemplified in beauty combined with concern for children and the nurturing of all in physical and emotional ways.

Jasmine

In India, this flower has long been called "Queen of the Night." It also symbolizes hope. In China, it is linked to the 'sweetness' of women. Many areas in the southern United States have 'night blooming jasmine' shrubs that emit this attractive fragrance into the environment during the blossom-time. Women of southern Asia (where jasmine originates) have long worn the delicate white flowers in their hair. Jasmine is also used to strengthen and ease the process of childbirth.

A famous woman who had her own jasmine gardens with servants dedicated to their cultivation was Cleopatra, Queen of Egypt. She was said to perfume the sails of her barge with this

Divine Feminine Handbook

potent fragrance. And she was known for her powerful allure that famously captured the attention and hearts of both Julius Caesar and Mark Antony.

From this image, we have a clue about the Jasmine personality characteristic: a confident, strong woman, and a bewitching seductress who knows how to attract what she requires. Jasmine releases inhibition and encourages playfulness.

Neroli

This essence has an interesting history. It comes from the blossoms of the orange tree which originated in China and the Far East. Oranges became known as 'golden apples.' In a famous legend, a 'golden apple' was tossed into a gathering of Greek goddesses by Eris, Goddess of Discord, with the comment, "for the fairest." A fierce contest of vanity began between these powerful women. Finally a young nobleman, Paris, was chosen to make the judgment and award the prize. Venus got Paris to choose her by promising him the love of the most beautiful woman in the world. Unfortunately, that woman was Helen of Troy, and it was their love that sparked the devastating Trojan War.

The aroma was said to be both euphoric and hypnotic and irresistible to men, garnering the nickname, 'man trap'. It was a fragrance used as a signature aroma, perfuming gloves and bath water with its beautiful scent, and was also famous for its healing and protective powers.

One of those healing powers involves the soothing of the stomach in times of anxiety. We could imagine that this quality, along with the powerful allure, caused the orange blossom to become a most popular flower in bridal bouquets.

The Neroli-type Divine Feminine is gentle, unassuming, and lovely with an air of otherworldly reserve.

93

Ylang Ylang

The aroma of Ylang Ylang is powerful and intensely sweet, but its unusual quality makes it very alluring to both men and women who are not fond of the more familiar flower aromas. Among its uses are relieving depression, anger and frustration. It can also reduce the stress associated with fear of sexual inadequacy. It can soothe palpitations from anxiety as well.

The Ylang Ylang-type is deeply passionate, fiery, temperamental, charismatic, feminine and seductive. They have a pronounced sense of self-confidence, allowing them to dress in bright clothing and eye-catching jewelry.

CHAPTER 10

Sacred Plant Medicine

*"Plants give us two things
pharmaceutical drugs cannot:
they give us nutrition and they detoxify."*
David Crowe

Plant Medicine

The earliest evidence of humans using plants medically dates back
to about 20,000 years ago. Paleolithic peoples in Lascaux, France
created cave paintings depicting herbal, aromatic medicines.

In the span of history, modern medicine is a very recent
invention. And yet our ancestors practiced medicine and treated
illness for thousands of years. Using knowledge passed down
through generations and nothing more than plants, they managed
to survive and thrive, despite living in extremely challenging
conditions.

A wealth of knowledge of natural remedies has been virtually
forgotten for decades, and scientists are just beginning to
rediscover the uses of the holistic spirituality of our ancestors

Plant Spirit Medicine is the shamans' way with plants. It

recognizes that plants have spirit and that spirit is the strongest medicine. Spirit can heal the deepest reaches of the heart and soul. Since the beginning of time, when the traditional shaman-healer turned to the plant world, she turned to the spirits of the plants. It was the spirits of the plants that healed her patients. The spirits were her friends, her teachers, and her allies.

When people refer to plant medicine these days, generally they're referring to the discovery that plants have certain chemicals that create changes in the biochemistry of the human body. Today, that is by far the most common approach to plant medicine in our society.

Today, the World Health Organization (WHO) estimates that 80 percent of the world's population still uses traditional remedies, including plants, as their primary health care tools. Meanwhile, the majority of new drugs (70 percent) introduced in the US are derived from natural products, primarily plants.

Unfortunately, the reverence for the use of medicinal plants in everyday life has largely been lost in the United States.

Herbs

Herbs can help support your health from a very basic level, just as foods do. In the late 1800s and early 1900s, you could walk into a drug store and find hundreds of herbal extracts for sale. Upwards of 90 percent of the population at that time knew how to use medicinal plants growing in their backyards to treat common illnesses and injuries; they had too, as this was virtually the only "medicine" available.

With the rise of what is now known as conventional allopathic medicine shortly before World War I, herbalism slowly fell out of favor and became to be thought of as folk medicine. Rather than viewing nature as the source of healing, as had been done for centuries, people began to view drugs and other "modern" healing methods as superior.

If you're looking for a powerful way to significantly boost your health, look no further than your own backyard. Growing your own fruits, vegetables and herbs may sound like a thing of the past, but it's more important now than ever to ensure that the food you eat is free of harmful chemical substances.

From marijuana to catnip, there are hundreds of remarkably common herbs, flowers, berries and plants that serve all kinds of important medicinal and health purposes that might surprise you:

- anti-inflammatory
- anti-fungal
- insect repellent
- antiseptic
- expectorant
- antibacterial
- detoxification
- fever reduction
- antihistamine
- pain relief

There are potent medicinal plants you're likely to find in the wild or even someone's backyard that can help with minor injuries, scrapes, bites and pains.

Essential Oils Are a Form of Plant Medicine

"The way to health is to have an aromatic bath and a scented massage every day" Hippocrates

For over 5,000 years, many different cultures have used these healing plant oils for a variety of health conditions. They are often used for relaxation, beauty care, home cleaning and most often used as natural medicine.

Essential oils are natural, aromatic volatile liquids found in shrubs, flowers, trees, roots, bushes, and seeds. Essential oils are highly concentrated oils that have a strong aroma. They can be thought of as nature's living energy.

By concentrating the oils of these plants, you are literally separating the most powerful healing compounds of a plant into a single oil. For instance, in order to get one single15ml bottle of rose essential oil, it takes 65 pounds of rose petals.

Today, essential oils are used for aromatherapy, nutritional supplements, massage therapy, diffusing, emotional health, personal care, perfumes, room sprays, household cleaning, repelling insects, and much more.

Essential oils are also a great natural pain remedy. They contain anti-inflammatory agents. They work so much better than OTC pain medication. They are a lot safer too.

Nature's Natural Antibiotics

So what does the term "natural antibiotic" really mean? Well, it is used to describe plants, herbs, or other natural substances that display very strong antimicrobial properties (meaning they can help fight viral, bacterial, fungal, or even parasitic infections).

It's important to know that these natural antibiotics have limitations and aren't always the right solution. As with any infection, it's highly important to talk to your physician and never self-diagnose and treat yourself without getting the proper diagnosis from a physician. This is gathering information so you can make an intelligent decision of how you wish to treat your condition. There are times when a pharmaceutical antibiotic can be life saving.

While antibiotics do have their place in modern medicine,

why not think about reaching for natural solutions provided by Mother Nature when you can? There are numerous studies which show that natural antibiotics are just as good as pharmaceuticals. In some cases, studies show that the natural antibiotics are even more effective than the pharmaceutical.

Keep in mind that studies usually don't use the raw plant. The scientists use strong extracts from the plants when doing their experiments. The results the scientists get may not reflect the results you'd get by eating the plant.

For example, garlic is one of the most well-known natural antibiotics. But it is the compound allicin in garlic which kills bacteria. You'd have to eat a lot of garlic to get enough allicin to treat a bacterial infection.

Likewise, most teas aren't potent enough to fight an infection. You could drink gallons of tea and still not make a dent in the bacterial population (though drinking fluids is important when sick!).

To make sure natural antibiotics are potent enough, you will need to buy them in tincture form or essential oils.

Natural Antibiotics:

- Garlic
- Cloves
- Cinnamon
- Hot Peppers
- Oregano
- Echinacea
- Colloidal Silver
- Probiotics
- Apple Cider Vinegar
- Cranberries
- Nettles
- Raw Honey

- Grapefruit Seed Extract
- Turmeric
- Extra Virgin Coconut Oil
- Ginger Root
- Thyme
- Goldenseal

CHAPTER 11

Creating Your Own Apothecary

*"Miracles are not contrary to nature, but
only contrary to what we know about nature."*

For decades the apothecary was where people went to be healed. It's where Wise Women kept their herbs and practiced their skills. The classic apothecary was very large. Today many of us do not have a place to create our own apothecary.

However creating your own little apothecary can be enjoyable and satisfying. As an Herbalist it's like our office. Start by gathering a bookcase, and use mason jars and other glass jars to fill with herbs and spices. Add your herbal books so you have a place to go for references. A mortar and pestle, and a few small bowls are handy for mixing herbal blends and teas. Try to label your jars of herbal formulas with the items name and date when made. I keep my essential oils in dark colored glass bottles, out of the light to keep them fresh.

Some other handy items to have: small cutting knife, small grater, small tins, and a journal to write down your formulas. Here is the list of items below for a well working apothecary:

- Bookcase(s) for shelving
- Work-table or desk with stool or chair to create items
- Mason Jars and glass jars to store herbs
- Small tins and jars to put herbal medicines in
- Labels
- Small knife for cutting up roots/herbs
- Mortar and Pestle
- Small grater – good for ginger, nutmeg, etc.
- Herbal books to find formulas
- Earthly items you like such as plants, gemstones, seashells
- A notebook or journal to write down your own formulas
- Essential oils and carrier oils
- Bees wax and butters, to make salves
- Vodka, at least over 80 proof (or 40% alcohol by volume) for making tinctures
- Small bowls to mix formulas
- Digital kitchen scale (weighing in grams)

Starting your own herbal collection at home doesn't have to be done in one fell swoop, it's a process. A process depending on what you and your family's needs are. I would break down what herbs to invest in by category and action, and then start trying them out yourself to see which are the most effective for you. Here are some basic botanical herbal actions to pick and choose from (although not nearly a complete list):

Herbs For Your Home Apothecary

Healthy Self = Heal Thy Self
Adaptogen (increases endurance and resistance to stress)
Ashwagandha, Holy Basil, Licorice, Milky Oat Tops, Nettle

Analgesics (Pain relieving)
Skullcap, ashwagandha

Antispasmodics (prevents and relieves spasms)
Chamomile, Peppermint, Skullcap, Yarrow, Wild Yam

Anti-inflammatory
Ashwagandha, Chamomile, Cinnamon, Holy Basil, Nettle, Turmeric, Yarrow

Anti-microbial
Chamomile, Elderberries, Yarrow, Ginger, Goldenseal

Bitters
Chamomile, Gentian, Dandelion leaf

Carminative (soothes digestion, relieves gas & bloating)
Fennel, Cardamom, Chamomile

Demulcent (to soothe inflamed tissues)
Marshmallow, Slippery Elm bark

Expectorant (increases the elimination of excess mucus)
Mullein, Wild Cherry, Thyme

Hepatic (liver protecting)
Burdock, Dandelion root, Turmeric, Reishi

Immune Stimulant (to acutely increase immune activity)
Echinacea root, Elderberries

Immune Modulator (to balance and support the immune system)
Astragalus, Reishi, Elderberries, Turmeric

Lymphatic
Calendula

Nutritive
Alfalfa, Nettle, Slippery Elm, Milky Oat, Reishi

Sedative/anxiolytic (calms the body and nervous system)
Chamomile, Ashwagandha, Skullcap, Passionflower, Valerian, Kava kava, Lemon balm

Stimulant (increases circulation and breaks through obstructions)
Ginger, Turmeric, Rosemary

If you have a well-stocked spice cupboard, you actually already have medicines at your fingertips.

Your apothecary is a place for you to practice your craft, to create herbal medicines, and a place where you enjoy being. It's so fun to create a little nook in your home with your remedies and herbs and spices and teas and tinctures to play with and actually use for good old fashioned preventative and acute care.

Build Your Tiny Apothecary

Essential Oils

- Frankincense
- Lavender
- Lemon
- Melaleuca
- Oregano
- Peppermint
- Wild Orange

Dried Herbs

- Arnica
- Calendula
- Chamomile
- Comfrey
- Elder flower
- Elderberry
- Lavender Flowers
- Lemon balm
- Marshmallow root
- Plaintain
- Yarrow

Raw Ingredients

- Beeswax
- Coconut Oil
- Fractionated Coconut Oil
- Castor Oil
- Olive Oil
- Shea Butter
- Redmond Clay Powder
- Liquid Castile Soap
- Vitamin E Oil
- Canned Coconut Milk
- Raw Honey

If you are not yet experienced in making herbal preparations begin your home apothecary with store bought high quality organic herbal products. In the meantime begin learning how to make and use your own, little by little you can replace the store bought with your own remedies.

Being self-reliant, knowledgeable, and prepared is something we Divine Feminine should constantly be engaging in and striving for.

SECTION TWO

Homemaking Skills

CHAPTER 12

Lost Homemaking Skills

A true home is one of the most sacred of places.
It is a sanctuary into which we flee
from the world's perils and alarms.

Dependency: The Way Most People Live Today

The way people live today is to be dependent on others. We depend on others to make and mend our clothes, to heal us when we are sick, to grow our food, to repair our homes and cars, to protect and defend us.

Is there anything we actually do ourselves? It really is unfortunate that we do almost nothing to sustain our own life. We have lost the skills that it takes to make it on our own; to feed ourselves, clothe ourselves, heal ourselves or take care of ourselves in most ways.

How did this happen? That can be summed up in two words: time and convenience. We stopped doing things ourselves because it took too much time. It became easier and more convenient to pay someone else to do these things, so we could move on to work more and play more.

After a while another ingredient was added to our demise: laziness. We got used to doing everything the quick and easy way, and we have become lazy. Why bake bread when you can buy a loaf at the corner store for a couple bucks. Why repair a pair of underwear when you can go to WalMart and pick up a six pack for $5?

What is Homemaking?

One of the most important jobs you'll ever have is caring for your home and family, yet there is very little education or training on basic homemaking skills. The reason why you create a home, is not for the sake of having a clean home, or decorated home, or impressing others. It's for your people to have a place where they can feel safe and loved. Every thing you do in and for your family to survive and thrive is included in your homemaking.

The definition of homemaking is "the creation and management of home as a pleasant place to live."

According to the Wikipedia definition, a homemaker is a person whose prime occupation is to care for their family and/ or home. The term homemaker is originally an American term, and while it has entered main stream English, it is not in common usage outside the United States.

Homemaking skills benefit us and our families in every area of our lives: spiritually, physically, intellectually, and emotionally. The good home is the rock foundation, the cornerstone of civilization. If our nation, is to endure, the home must be safeguarded, strengthened, and restored to its rightful importance.

How Can I Enjoy Homemaking?

Dishes, meals, and laundry can feel mundane day after day, but when you remember the reasons WHY you are doing all of those things, that helps you enjoy it so much more. It also helps to create schedules and routines so that homemaking is not so overwhelming.

Homemaking is whatever you make of it. Every day brings satisfaction along with some work which may be frustrating, routine, and unchallenging. But it is the same in any vocation.

Cooking From Scratch

From the earliest days as hunter-gathers to the first domestication of plants, it was women who stoked the first hearths, stirred the first pots, brewed the first beer, and baked the first bread.

Women's role in food production was considered sacred. Long before food was bought and sold for profit, no act of food production, from harvesting, growing, preparing, preserving, storing, cooking or baking was left unblessed by women's prayers, rituals, and devotions.

Women no longer gather communally to harvest with prayer and song, but shop hurried and alone in corporate superstores, and the kitchen is a place where we consume the processed and fast food that suit our busy lifestyles.

Do you know how to cook from scratch? I mean real cooking like baking your own bread or making cookies and cakes without a mix. Can you make pasta without a machine? Can you make homemade gravy? People used to cook every single meal from scratch with real food like potatoes, tomatoes, eggs, milk and real butter. They did not get up in the morning and pull a breakfast burrito out of the freezer. They made real oatmeal from oats and toast from home baked bread.

The practice of cooking from scratch is pretty rare these days. You will not find too many people that do it, but the people that do will generally be healthier and happier. If you don't know how to cook, it is a very good idea to learn because that breakfast burrito may not always be available for you to buy or you may not have the money, in the future.

Home cooking allows people to come together. Making meals at home just seems to make everyone happy. Sitting down and eating a meal that you created together is a daily celebration of life. Even if your family consists of you and your furry friend, love yourself enough to prepare healthy meals for the both of you.

It's time to bring love back into the kitchen now, you don't have to wait for a disaster or emergency situation to begin preparing meals from scratch. Cooking is as simple as following a recipe. Don't over complicate it.

Food Preservation - Fermenting, Dehydrating, Freezing, Canning

Food preservation used to be a part of everyday life, in most families. This was before we had stores on every corner with all kinds of food trucked in year round and the money to buy it. It used to be that the end of the summer was the busiest time in any household as the family canned, dehydrated or froze the fruits and veggies of their labor, so they would have food to eat all winter.

What would you do if someone gave you a whole bushel of tomatoes, green beans or corn? Would you have any idea what to do with the excess that you could not eat before it spoiled?

Furthermore, what would you do, if something happened and all those corner stores could no longer get any food to sell you? What if all the sudden you were unable to buy food anywhere?

What if you lost your job and didn't have much money to buy food? What would you do?

These are questions that help you understand why it is a good idea to learn how to preserve food for yourself and your family. Canning, fermenting, dehydrating and freezing food is not terribly difficult to do, but it is a skill that must be learned and done right, if you want to be prepared. Prepared for what? For an earthquake, flood, or any type of disaster that will disrupt the delivery of food to stores. It is also good to have extra food on hand for other reasons, such as unexpected company, job loss of the primary provider, or another pandemic.

Mending Clothing or Sewing Garments from Scratch

What would you do, if you put on a pair of socks, and your toe poked through a hole? Or if a belt loop ripped off your favorite jeans. What if you got a gorgeous dress for a great price, but it was three inches too long? What would you do?

I can tell you what most people, today, would do: throw the sock away, safety pin the belt loop, and take the dress to the alteration shop to be shortened.

Fifty years ago we would have darned the sock, sewn the belt loop back on, and shortened the dress ourselves. When did this change? Why did it change? Sewing and basic mending used to be taught in school in Home Economics as a basic part of our education. It is a real shame that so few people know how to perform even the most basic of repairs. Imagine the money you could save, if you could mend small holes in socks, underwear, jeans and pants. Sewing is very worthwhile to learn.

Line Drying Clothes

This may be the simplest start on the whole list. We are just too darn busy to be bothered with drying our clothes outdoors. Let me tell you though, you haven't lived until you have slept on some fresh line dried sheets in the summer sun, really, it's true. Oh, and don't forget the fact that it really does save on electricity.

First Aid - From Skinned Knees to Heart Attacks

First Aid is a skill that is so important that you can literally save someone's life, if you know it. I find it amazing that First Aid is not taught more in schools. I am not talking CPR, or the Heimlich Manuver, both of which are important to know; I am talking about what to do if someone cuts their hand very badly while chopping vegetables. Or a dog attacks someone and bites them severely. Or you see a bad car accident and people are bleeding and hurt. Would you know what to do?

Sometimes what you do right after an injury occurs makes the difference in whether or not they keep their finger or limb, or even their life. It is very important to know the basic tenants of first aid for cuts, bruises, burns and trauma. The best way to learn these is to take a class. However, if you cannot take a class, there are many books and videos that can teach you almost as well. It is not difficult to learn first aid, and it could be such a huge help to someone that is hurt.

Basic Tool Skills - Using Hand Tools and Power Tools

If you aren't already familiar, you need to introduce yourself to tools. A hammer, screwdriver, pliers, measuring tape, wrench and other hand tools are easy to use and with a little practice, you can handle them like a pro. Driving a nail straight, or turning a screw can be mastered with time, all you have to do is to pick one up and go for it.

Learning to handle common tools is important. Doing simply repairs around the house can save you money. Shingles blow off your roof? Find them and nail them back on. Your downspout falls off your gutter? Climb your ladder, or borrow one, and put it back on. There is no need to call a handyman and pay ridiculous fees for simple jobs you can do yourself. Buy yourself some tools and do it yourself, and if you don't know how, there's always YouTube.

Home Management

Home management is planning, controlling and evaluating the use of resources of the family for the purpose of attaining family goals.

In simple terms, home management is a family working together for common purposes, the forming of plan of action, the sharing of responsibilities, the organized and controlled use of available resources. It involves the homemaker's managerial ability, her interest, capacity to motivate the other members of the family, to work to achieve a common goal for the development of the family. Effective management enhances the chances of achieving goals by making wise decisions and proper utilization of resources.

Having home management skills are important and they will help create the home that you want and love. Creating a home management plan will help you pull together all the different areas you need to consider when looking after a home and family.

Spending Time With Your Family

Having time to do the fun stuff as a family is very important and often overlooked. You won't get the time again with family and making this time a priority will improve communication and relationships. Making family time special will allow you to make your family feel important and part of the process of home life.

It's about connecting with your family and making memories that are special and important so they can look back on them when times are tough. Making your family a priority will ensure that you are all on the same page and able to communicate with each other when life throws one of those unexpected curve balls.

How To Deal With Home Organization

You need to have some sort of organization systems in your home. There will be more than one system as you will need different systems for the different areas of your home.

The most important thing to think about when organizing is finding homes for the things you and your family members own. This gives them a place where they belong and they have somewhere to go. Without having homes for the" things" it's difficult to keep your home looking tidy because know one will know where to put things when they have finished using them.

Getting your home to the point where your home is decluttered and everything has its own home takes time. You have to learn the skills required when it comes to organizing. It isn't going to happen overnight, it will take time and practice to get it right.

I can still hear these words ringing in my ears; "Everything has a place. Put everything back in its place when you are finished with it."

Without a clear organizational system, you won't be able to

keep up your home's cleanliness because you'll have too much stuff collecting dust.

Delegate

What do you do, that someone else could do instead? Who else in the house could take on a task? Companies invest time and money in staff training because they believe it will improve their productivity and profit margins. Why not do it at home where "profit" equates to more time?

If there are things that can be better done by others or things that are not so important, consider delegating. This takes a load off and you can focus on the important tasks. A partner and children are always great people to delegate chores to. If they live in the house they have a responsibility to care for it and themselves, but you have to teach them.

Know How to Balance Your Checking Account

Take 15 minutes to balance your checking account, stay on top of your budget and avoid bounced checks, overdraft fees and embarrassment when your debit card is denied.

Know How to Make a Budget

You can have a choice in where your money goes and you do not have to be stressed about your finances. When you are aware of how your money is being spent it is easier to be in control of it.

- keeping, recording, and organizing receipts
- recording any expenses
- reconciling accounts

- paying bills
- assessing budgets
- sorting and filing paperwork

Calendar

Keep a calendar or planner to keep track of all the appointments, school activities, and important information. Review your planner each morning so you never forget something crucial. Get in the habit of writing in it regularly.

If you're out and you make a meeting or appointment, create an alert on your phone so you remember to write it down when you get home.

Dealing With Mail

Unless you deal with mail as soon as it comes into the home it can quickly take over your home, but also there is the possibility of missing some important information or even missing the payment on a bill which can cause late payment fees.

You have to create a system that allows you to deal with mail when it turns up so that you aren't stuffing it into a drawer and forgetting about it. Or, worse still just throwing it away without checking what's inside. You have to create a system that works for you and your family.

Take into consideration who opens the mail, who pays the bills and what systems you need to have in place for organizing the mail you need to keep and shredding the items you don't need to keep.

Creating Routines And Schedules

Without routines you will struggle to get things done. They are the most important thing that you can set up for yourself and encourage your children to have routines too. This will help them to get the tasks they need to do done too.

Having a morning and an evening routine will help you get things done on autopilot and without really thinking about them. They also make the morning start off better as you are more prepared for the day. It's a way to trick yourself into getting things that you need to do regularly. You complete the task at a certain time in the day and then it's done.

Habits can take a while to set up so it's important to track your routines that you are trying to build. You should start to remember your routines within a week or two but it can take weeks for them to become automatic so be patient with yourself.

Chores

The motto in our home is "You live here – you help out." It's not just one person's responsibility to keep the house clean and stay on top of household chores. Each person in the house should help to keep the home in order. This can take the load off of you having to do it all yourself, because nowhere does it say it's only your responsibility. You may be a homemaker but you aren't a maid.

Housekeeping Skills

Housekeeping includes performing such activities as, sweeping, mopping, vacuuming, and dusting your living space, planning and preparing meals, doing laundry, and maintaining a yard and the exterior of your home.

Whether your living space is large or small, humble or extravagant, keep it in good repair and beautify your home, your yard, farm, and business. Repair the fences. Clean up and paint where needed. Keep your lawns and your gardens well-groomed. Whatever your circumstance, let your premises reflect orderliness, beauty, and happiness.

Imagine that you are opening your front door and walking inside your home. What do you see, and how do you feel? Is it a place of love, peace, and refuge from the world? Is it clean and orderly? As you walk through the rooms of your home, do you see uplifting images? Is your bedroom or sleeping area a place for personal space and alone time? Is your gathering area or kitchen a place where food is prepared and enjoyed together, allowing uplifting conversation and family time?

Meal Planning

Knowing what you are having to eat each night is important in any household. But when you have a family making sure that everyone is getting a good balanced diet and on a budget is important. It's not as simple as rummaging through the freezer right before you need to prepare the evening meal, it's about planning what you can eat and getting a variety into your diet that takes into account favorite meals and home cooking.

Cooking meals at home is something that seems to be declining, but it's a skill that you should develop as it is healthier and can save you a lot of money and this is always important when managing a home. If you don't believe me look over your bank statement from last month and add up how much money you spent eating out; fast food, dinning out, lunch breaks, coffee houses, etc.

CHAPTER 13

Cooking From Scratch

If you don't know how to cook you don't know how to take care of yourself.

Our ancestors knew how to cook because if you were hungry, you had to cook. Today, many people don't have even basic cooking skills. At the end of the day, if you don't know how to cook you don't know how to take care of yourself.

Cooking from scratch is a very conscious choice for me. Partly because it's far healthier, partly because it allows us to use the food we're growing ourselves, but the biggest reason? It's about quality of life. Food is appreciated more and tastes better when it's cooked from scratch and made with love. A splendid meal is only made possible with delicious ingredients. When you touch the dough and smell the bread it truly feeds the soul.

Cooking is an art. The process of preparing a meal is creative, therapeutic and is a gift to those you share the meal with. The table is a place to learn about others, grow closer in your relationships and pour out your hearts. Be inspired to nourish your body and mind with whole foods and a home-cooked meal.

Cooking from scratch can sometimes be overwhelming.

Cooking from scratch is not grilling a hamburger on the grill. It can be using a recipe or just cooking the way that comes naturally to you. It can help you eat healthier, save money, and reduce your dependence on the grocery store.

If you're a beginner cook and want to make healthy food for your family, you may feel overwhelmed because learning to cook takes time and patience. Using a plant-based cookbook will help you learn the skills you need to get started cooking from scratch. Convenience foods are great, but when all you do to prepare dinner day in and day out is open a package, something important is lost.

If you're choosing to cook from scratch so you have healthier food, it makes sense to find some convenience foods that you can still rely on once in a while. Yes, they're still packaged, and yes, they still have a few ingredients that aren't ideal. But organic and natural packaged foods are better than conventional packaged and convenience foods.

Since you are relying on these packaged foods much less frequently, you probably can afford the organic ones the few times you need them. Having these as a backup while you learn to cook from scratch can save you a lot of stress. It can also help avoid last-minute dinners out.

If you feel like cooking from scratch 7 days a week is too much then start with one meal, one day. Ease yourself into cooking from scratch. Get some cookbooks with pictures that look amazing. Build upon your one meal, once a week until you're doing every meal that way. Then you'll probably find your own reasons that you love this way of preparing meals.

Amazing Reasons You Need To Be Cooking From Scratch

It is a Vintage Skill that Needs Revival

Once upon a time all food was prepared the long way. Convenience foods are still pretty new, if we consider the history of food preparation, but they seem to have taken the prime seat at our tables. The art of cooking is a vintage skill that needs to be preserved for the generations to come.

Your Health Will Thank You

I don't want to go into a long lecture about the crap that is in the food you get through a drive thru, out of a box or even from the freezer section of the store. Most of us are aware that these foods are filled with chemical additives that have no place in the human body. When you start cooking, really cooking, your health improves naturally.

You Can Make Informed Choices

The best part about cooking from scratch is that YOU choose the ingredients, not some company with profit as its main objective. This means you can grow what you want to eat, organically. Or you can purchase from local farmers and ranchers that you want to support and give your money to.

You Know Your Food

This ties into making informed choices. When you are cooking real food, you know exactly what you are eating. I know most of my veggies because I grew them from little seeds. It is amazing to spend time in the kitchen with real food that is fresh, local and sustainable.

It Can Bring Your Closer to Your Loved Ones

There is something about preparing a meal for the people you love. There is also something equally exciting about having a meal lovingly prepared for you. Meals cooked with fresh ingredients are meant to be enjoyed at a table with your friends and family, whenever possible. Not in front of a screen. Shared meals gives you time to talk and reflect with your loved ones and that will ultimately bring you closer.

Saves You Money

If you're buying all your food from an expensive big-chain health food grocery, you're not likely to save money. Their stores are filled with organic convenience food that is pretty pricey. But if you shop the edges of the store where fresh foods are, you'll likely save money on healthy options. Of course even bigger savings can happen in producing your own foods and/or buying locally from farmers.

Expand Your Palate

Once you "cleanse" your palate of junk food the good stuff just begins to taste better. And when you grow delicious heirloom vegetables in your backyard it is like tasting them for the very first time. You actually start to crave a fresh salad or your home grown tomato sandwich.

Learning How To Cook

Learning how to cook at home can be liberating, fun and at times overwhelming. If you want to learn to be a better cook, you need to start by sticking to a recipe. You may think that you can make changes and substitutes or not measure your ingredients, but until you're confident that you know what you're doing, don't stray from the recipe.

Follow each step in the order it's written. Measure and put things in at the right time. Cook it for the stated amount of time.

If you make too many changes, the recipe may not turn out. Good cooks and chefs can improvise; beginner cooks should stick to the recipe.

Buy A Quality Knife

I can't tell you how important this is. If you're doing all of your cutting with a dull knife, that's not only inefficient, it's dangerous. It's time to upgrade. But you don't really need one of those chopping blocks full of knives. All you need is one good chef's knife. And by good, I mean a high-quality, sharp chef's knife. A high-quality chef's knife makes all the difference when you're prepping your food.

Imagine having just ONE really high-quality knife instead of a block of several knives that just work okay. It's like an all-in-one tool you can use it for most everything. In fact, most chefs do.

Give Yourself a Cookbook Challenge

Did you ever watch the movie, Julie and Julia? Picking a cookbook and working your way through it, recipe by recipe, is a great way to grow in your cooking skills.

All you have to do is pick a basic cookbook (or a cookbook that demonstrates the type of cooking you want to learn) and start cooking.

You could give yourself 30 days to cook 30 recipes or cook from one chapter a month. You could go about your challenge in any number of ways. You could even find some friends to do it with you and post your progress in a Facebook group or on Instagram.

125

Learn From Friends

If you have a friend who is a great cook, ask her or him to teach you. It would be a great way to spend time together and learn how to cook.

Get together once a week for a cooking lesson. Each week or month you could concentrate on a certain type of dish: appetizers, plant based, raw, vegetarian or desserts. Or maybe you want to learn a certain cooking method like Instant Pot cooking or one pot meals.

Look for those friends for whom cooking comes naturally, and just ask. Most likely, they will be honored and thrilled to teach you.

Watch Cooking Shows

No matter what you think about foodies or the Food Network, watching cooking shows is a great way to learn how to cook. And there are so many choices.

You can learn how to cook. And with all of these ideas, you can improve your cooking skills little by little. Don't be overwhelmed. Just pick one or two things from the list and start there. You've totally got this.

Cooking For One

Here's a trick when you need inspiration in your cooking-for-one routine, especially when you arrive home in the evenings and heating a pizza seems like the easiest way to go. For about the same amount of time it would take for your oven to preheat and that frozen pizza to bake, you can put together a healthy, vegetable-intense dinner that tastes delicious and fills you up. What's the secret? Cook a pot of rice or potatoes on Sunday night and use it throughout the week. Make a soup, cut up veggies, make a homemade salad dressing for the week.

The rice bowl is perhaps the perfect Cooking for One dish. Besides the fact that it is assembled in individual portions, it offers variety and versatility and a fantastic opportunity to clean out the refrigerator.

Rice bowls are different than fried rice in that the flavor components are arranged on a bed of rice rather than mixed or stir-fried in. This gives the eater the opportunity to customize each mouthful, pulling a little here and there from each of toppings. The rice bowl is easily customizable, influenced only by your appetite and what's in the refrigerator. It can be vegan, vegetarian or meat-centric. A fried or poached egg is a classic topping and if the yolk is left runny, it will sauce the rice and add a lovely richness to the dish.

Make a large salad, without dressing, to eat during the week. Making your own meals doesn't always have to involve any cooking at all. As well as eating raw veggies and salads, try uncooked probiotic foods, those containing "good" bacteria, such as yogurt, sauerkraut, soft cheese, or vegetables fermented in brine, for quick and healthy snacks or side dishes.

There are simple meals that need little work. Beat an egg; heat some broth; chop a couple of carrots. Voila, egg drop soup.

Sometimes little snacks can add up to a nice meal, if you take a hint from the Mediterranean mezze approach. Try a scoop of hummus with a few pita wedges, a wedge of feta, some baby spinach drizzled with olive oil and a quick squirt of lemon, a few roasted red peppers from a jar, a handful of almonds. This lovely meal can come together in about five minutes and is delicious, nutritious and festive!

CHAPTER 14

DIY Milk Alternatives

While we were all brought up believing a glass of milk was a great way to get calcium and protein, it turns out that milk doesn't have to come from a cow. There are a lot of health benefits to drinking non-dairy milk, and for some people, it's the only option as they're lactose intolerant or have allergies or sensitivities to dairy.

Dairy is a tremendous mucus producer. When the protein of another animal is introduced into one's immune system, an allergic/immune response is created in many places in the body. A common reaction to such an assault by a foreign protein in our immune system is an outpouring of mucus from the nasal and throat membranes. The resulting mucus flow can create the chronic runny noses, persistent sore throats, hoarseness, bronchitis, and the recurrent ear infections that plague so many children and their parents. No age is exempt, and milk allergy may be first detected during adolescence or adulthood.

Excess mucus caused by milk can harden to form a coating on the inner wall of the intestines, hindering the absorption of nutrients and possibly leading to chronic fatigue. If a child has food sensitivities to milk, the symptoms can include eczema, bloating, runny nose, chronic ear infections, stomach problems and asthma. Even things like kidney and bladder problems.

More and more people are discovering sensitivities to dairy products. Some of us may not have any dairy allergies, but we realize how much better we feel when limiting dairy in our diets.

Plant based milk is not meant to replace breast milk or baby formula, it will not meet your babies nutritional needs, but it works great for cooking, on cereal, beverages and most other things you would normally use milk for.

A great reason to try non dairy milk is the ease in making it at home, it only takes a few minutes to make and it suites a plant based diet. A variety of nuts, seeds, and legumes can be used to your liking in homemade plant-based milk.

What Are Plant-Based Milks And Nut Milks?

Plant-based milks are made by blending a nut, seed, grain, or fruit (coconut) with filtered water. Then, milks are flavored and sweetened, if desired. And, to make milks shelf-stable, they are often pasteurized and contain additives and preservatives.

There is a wide range of plant-based milks available at health food stores and grocery stores. And they range from pure simple boutique products made in small batches with very few ingredients, to mass-produced products containing a lot of additives, preservatives, and sweeteners.

As a general rule, the cheaper the product, the more chemicals it contains. Pure organic plant-based milks tend to be a lot more expensive. With plant-based milks, you do get what you pay for.

I generally use commercial milks as little as possible. Instead, I prefer to make my own homemade nut milks, seed milks, grain milks, and coconut milk.

The benefits of homemade plant-based milk:

- fresher
- taste better
- free from additives and preservatives
- you have complete control over the integrity of the milk

You can determine the:

- flavor
- texture
- sweetness
- you can make them more digestible by neutralizing the enzyme inhibitors and activating the full nutrient potential by soaking the ingredients before you blend them

Do You Need A High-Speed Blender To Make Nut Milk?

A high-speed blender yields the best results when making plant based milks. They really pulverize the nuts, seeds, and grains for a smooth texture. Having said that, you can make milk in any conventional full-size blender.

To Strain Or Not To Strain?

Whole, unstrained milks retain all of the nutrients of the whole food, so they offer the most nutritional benefits. However, they can have a gritty texture, and are not palatable for most people. Unstrained milks also don't do well when used in some recipes. It is best to strain plant-based milks for use in some recipes.

Milks that do not need straining:

- cashews
- macadamia
- pecans
- coconut

These nuts yield milks that are incredibly smooth when made in a high- speed blender. So, they do not need to be strained. However, if you're using a conventional blender you will need to strain them to achieve a smooth consistency.

Nut Milks

- almond milk
- walnut milk
- pecan milk
- hazelnut milk
- Brazil nut milk
- cashew milk
- macadamia milk

Seed Milks

- white sesame seed milk
- hemp seed milk
- sunflower seed milk
- pumpkin seed milk

Grain Milks

- rice milk
- oat milk

Fruit Milks

- coconut milk

Recipes

Homemade Raw Nut Milk

Homemade nut milk is a great dairy-free alternative and is also very cost effective comparatively to buying store bought nut milks. You can use cashew, hazelnut, pecan, almond, brazil, macadamia and walnut.

Main Ingredients:

As a general rule, use 2:1 water to nuts. I like my nut milk a little more rich at that ratio. You can also do a 3:1 or even 4:1 ratio for a lighter nut milk.

- 2 cups of raw, organic, soaked nuts
- 4 cups of filtered water

Directions:

- Soak all nuts separately in filtered water for a minimum of 4 hours, or ideally overnight in the refrigerator. Soaking the nuts makes a "softer" nut for blending. It also increases the nut enzyme activity (for easier digestion and assimilation) and increases nutrient content levels, as well as reduces anti-nutrient compounds such as lectins.
- Once the raw nuts have soaked, drain the water and add the raw nuts to a blender with fresh filtered water.
- Blend the raw nuts and water for 1 minute.
- Once blended, filter, through a sieve or nut milk bag.
- Once it's done filtering through, add your nut milk to a glass jar and keep refrigerated for plain, unsweetened nut milk. If you're looking to sweeten and flavor your nut milks, here are a few different options below:

Options for non-plain nut milk:

For all ingredient options below, simply take your unsweetened nut milk and add each desired flavoring to your blender. Blend for 10-15 seconds on low, or until all ingredients are incorporated nicely.

Option #1: **Low Carb & No-Added Sugar Nut Milk**

- 1/8 – 1/4 teaspoon stevia powder (depending on how sweet you want- stevia is potent!)
  1/2 tablespoon vanilla extract
  1/2 teaspoon cinnamon

Option #2: **Low-Glycemic Sugar Nut Milk**

- 1 tablespoon Coconut Nectar
  1/2 tablespoon vanilla extract
  1/2 teaspoon cinnamon

Optional Ingredient #1: **Coconut Milk**

If you're looking to try a coconut milk/nut milk combo, take a 1/2 cup to 1 cup of organic canned 'lite' coconut milk (or water down 1/4 cup to 1/2 cup regular canned coconut milk) depending on how much coconut flavor you want. Simply combine in the blender with whatever nut milk ingredients you choose. It tastes richer, as well as extends the total amount per batch.

Golden Cashew:

- 1-inch piece fresh turmeric, peeled
- 1 tablespoon maple syrup, or to taste
- 1/8 teaspoon ground cinnamon
- pinch or two ground turmeric, if desired
- pinch sea salt

Cocoa Hazelnut:

- 4 pitted dates, coarsely chopped, or to taste
- 2 tablespoons unsweetened cocoa powder
- pinch sea salt

Maple Pecan:

- 2 tablespoons maple syrup, or to taste
- pinch sea salt

Once you finish your nut milks, simply keep refrigerated in a glass jar. Homemade nut milks will usually keep in the fridge for a good 4-5 days.

Also, don't throw away your nut pulp. You can use these to make nut flours, muffins, crackers and other baked goods. Place nut pulps in a zip lock bags and label each and freeze them to use at a later time.

Strawberry Syrup For Strawberry Milk (Dye and Refined Sugar Free!)

Ingredients:

- 2 cups strawberries frozen or fresh
- 1 cup water
- 1/2 cup honey add more if you want a sweeter syrup

Instructions:

- Put everything in a small sauce pan and bring the ingredients to a simmer for 15 minutes. Stir occasionally squishing the strawberries along the way.
- Strain the syrup. Be sure to squish the strawberries with the back of your spoon to get all the juice out. (Save the

left behind strawberries to put in your morning smoothie, or top on vanilla ice cream.)
- Use 3-4 tablespoons of syrup per 1 cup of milk

Recipe Notes:

This recipe makes enough for 2-3 cups of milk. Double or triple the recipe if needed. Homemade strawberry syrup will keep in the fridge for 7-10 days, or can be stored in the freezer for 6 months.

Coffee Shop Worthy Caramel Vanilla Bean Hazelnut Milk

Decadent, luxurious, and totally splurge-worthy, this homemade hazelnut milk is fit for a high end coffee shop and it pairs perfectly in a cup of coffee or black tea. I use a mix of soaked hazelnuts and almonds, but feel free to use all hazelnuts if you prefer. It's lightly flavored with notes of caramel (from Medjool dates), cinnamon, and a whole vanilla bean and I imagine you could turn it into a chocolate hazelnut milk quite easily by adding a bit of cacao powder.

Ingredients:

- 3/4 cup raw hazelnuts
- 1/4 cup raw almonds
- 3 1/2 cups water
- 2 1/2-3 pitted Medjool dates, to taste
- 1 vanilla bean, roughly chopped
- 1/2 teaspoon cinnamon
- tiny pinch of fine grain sea salt (optional)

Directions:

- Place hazelnuts and almonds in a bowl and cover with water. It's preferred to soak them overnight (for 8-12 hours) in the water, but you can get away with soaking for 1-2 hours in a pinch.
- Rinse and drain the soaked hazelnuts and almonds. Place nuts into a blender along with water, pitted dates, vanilla bean, cinnamon, and salt (if using).
- Cover and blend on highest speed for 1 minute or so.
- Place a nut milk bag over a large bowl and slowly pour the milk mixture into the bag. Gently squeeze the bottom of the bag to release the milk. This process can take 3-5 minutes, so be patient. You should be left with about 1 cup of pulp in the bag. See my tips below on using the leftover pulp.
- Rinse out blender and pour the milk back in. Now, pour it easily into a Mason jar and secure with lid. Chill in the fridge. It will stay fresh for 2-3 days. Give the jar a good shake before enjoying.
- Drink it alone, use it in cereal or smoothies, make hot oatmeal, and as a creamer in coffee or tea.

Tips:

1) If your dates or vanilla bean are dry/stiff, soak in water to soften before use. You can also use another sweetener of your choice like maple syrup instead of dates. Same goes for vanilla, feel free to use vanilla extract for a more subtle vanilla flavor.
2) Ideas for using leftover pulp: stir into oatmeal or muffin batter, add to smoothies, make crackers, or you can even dehydrate it and then blend it up to make hazelnut meal. You can freeze it for a later use too.

3) You might be wondering; If I don't have a nut milk bag can I use a fine mesh sieve? Yes you can. I don't find the milk gets as smooth compared to using a nut milk bag, but if you strain it several times, it comes out decent. Also, feel free to try a cheesecloth (you can even line the sieve with a layer of cheesecloth).

Pumpkin Seed Milk

Pumpkin seed milk is a fun way to include these nutrient-rich seeds into your diet. Pumpkin seeds are one of the highest plant-based sources of protein containing all essential amino acids. A handful of pepitas makes up almost half of the recommended daily allowance of protein. Pepitas are also a rich source of iron, with one cup delivering almost half of the RDA of iron. Pepitas are also a good source of zinc, for bone health. Pumpkin seeds are also a good source of calcium, magnesium, manganese, potassium, phosphorus, and copper; as well as Vitamins A, B and E.

Loaded with heart-healthy unsaturated fats and omega-3 and omega-6 fatty acids, pumpkin seeds are anti-inflammatory avengers that help regulate blood pressure and cholesterol for heart health. They also contain tryptophan to alleviate anxiety and aid sleep.

Purchase raw pumpkin seeds from a supplier with a high turn over to ensure maximum freshness and quality, and store in a sealed glass container in the fridge, and consume within a couple of months. Or scoop seeds out of pumpkins and dehydrate the seeds.

Pumpkin seeds have a subtle sweet and nutty flavor. Some pumpkin seeds have a creamy husk, but the majority of pepitas are flat and dark green in color, so your milk will have a green tinge to it.

Pumpkin seed milk has a small amount of texture. You don't

really need to strain it. In fact, you'll get more nutritional benefit if you don't strain it. However, for a silky smooth texture like a commercial-style milk for use in recipes, strain it. Use the smooth pulp for crackers, savory balls, and crusts.

Pumpkin seed milk does have a distinctive flavor. I sweeten it and add a bit of vanilla extract to lift and brighten the flavor. Pumpkin seed milk is delicious mixed with some carrot juice and a pinch of cinnamon.

Unsweetened Pumpkin Seed Milk

Ingredients:

- 1 cup raw pumpkin seeds, soaked for 8 hours
- 3 cups filtered water
- Pinch of Celtic sea salt

Sweetened Milk (Unsweetened Milk, Plus Below):

- 1/4 cup pitted dates (or 2 tablespoons pure maple syrup), plus more to taste
- 1 teaspoon natural vanilla extract
- 1 tablespoon sunflower lecithin (optional)

Instructions:

- To soak the pumpkin seeds, place them in a glass or ceramic bowl or large glass jar, and cover with filtered water. Add 1 teaspoon Celtic sea salt and splash of fresh lemon juice or apple cider vinegar, cover the container with a breathable kitchen towel, and allow to soak at room temperature for 8 hours.
- Drain, and discard the soaking liquid. Rinse the pumpkin seeds several times to remove the anti-nutrients and enzyme inhibitors.

- Throw the rinsed pumpkin seeds, water, and salt in your blender, and blast on high for 30 to 60 seconds, until the nuts are completely pulverized. Use whole milk to maximize nutrition. Or strain for a smoother, more commercial-style milk for use in recipes.
- To strain, place a nut milk bag or knee-high piece of sheer nylon hosiery over the opening of a glass bowl, jar or jug. Pour the milk into the bag, twisting the bag closed, and gently squeezing it to pass the liquid through. Empty the pulp aside. You can dehydrate this for use in smoothies or to make crusts. Or use to make a quick easy body scrub.
- Rinse your blender container, and pour the strained milk back in. Add the vanilla, sweetener, and any flavorings, and blast again, until smooth and creamy.
- Store the milk in a sealed container in the fridge. Activated pumpkin seed milk (made with soaked pumpkin seeds) will keep for 2 to 3 days in a very cold fridge. Un-soaked pumpkin seed milk will keep for about 5 days.

How to Make Oat Milk

Making delicious oat milk is easy! But if you have made other plant-based milks in the past, a word to the wise: it is NOT like making almond milk, where you wring as much liquid as you can out of a nut milk bag. In this recipe, your goal is to squeeze and press the mixture as little as possible. Otherwise, it will end up slimy and grainy. Here's my method:

Blend:

First, add the oats and filtered water to a powerful blender (I use a Vitamix) and blend for 30 seconds, until the water looks creamy and white. For the best texture, be careful not to over-blend!

Strain:

Next, place a fine mesh strainer over a large bowl and pour the oat milk through it. Some liquid may pool at the bottom of the strainer. That's ok! Discard this liquid and any oat pulp below it. DO NOT try to press the pulp to get more liquid through the strainer, as it will make the milk slimy and gritty.

Strain again (optional). For extra-smooth oat milk, strain the liquid twice, discarding the leftover pulp both times. This step is optional, but it will yield the smoothest final texture.

Chill:

Chill, and enjoy! I like my oat milk best when it's cold from the fridge. Unlike other dairy-free milks, don't shake it when you go to use it. Instead, allow any leftover oat pulp to settle at the bottom of the container, and pour the creamy milk off the top.

Oat Milk

Ingredients:

- 1/2 cup whole rolled oats
- 3 cups water
- 2 teaspoons maple syrup
- ½ teaspoon vanilla extract
- c teaspoon sea salt

Instructions:

- Combine the oats, water, maple syrup, vanilla, and salt in a blender and blend for 30 seconds.
- Place a fine mesh strainer over a large bowl and strain the milk without pushing any excess pulp through the strainer. This will create a creamier texture that's not gritty or gummy.
- Add more maple syrup, to taste, if desired. Chill overnight. If you want to drink your oat milk right away, I recommend adding ice, it's flavor is best when well chilled.

- As the oat milk sits in the fridge, natural separation will occur. You can shake it, if you like, but I like it's texture best when I leave pulp at the bottom and pour off the top.

CHAPTER 15

Sprouts

Most people consume seeds (nuts, grains, legumes) that are in a hibernation phase, either raw or cooked, when their nutrients are locked up tight by de-activators such as phytic acid and other enzyme inhibitors. These dormant seeds are more difficult to digest and can block nutrient absorption and uptake. In order to maximize the nourishing potential of seeds (nuts, grains, legumes), we need to unlock them with a simple and common-sense key: give them life. Allow them to grow, and they will repay you in spades.

There's a whole world to choose from, with a huge range of textures and flavors, from amaranth, brassicas and popcorn to pea shoots and sunflower. Once we've got them growing, we can use them in everything we would a lettuce or fresh vegetable, soups, stir fry, salads, sandwiches, stackers, omelets, and wraps.

Sprouting seeds is one of the easiest and best things you can do for your health. Seeds that sprout are also some of the best food items to add to your food storage for emergency preparedness. They will give you fresh greens and protein. Wheat sprouts and wheat grass are a great way to get some fresh greens (and the nutrients that come with them) into your food storage.

Sprouts are one of mother nature's super foods. They are rich in nutrients, they have a ton more enzymes than most other raw food, they are high in protein, they help with weight loss, they are a good source of energy. True health comes from living foods. Eating sprouts can make you feel alive and energized.

The nutritional uniqueness of sprouts is that they are virtually still growing when we eat them. Unlike most produce, which slowly begins losing vitamins and minerals when harvested, the nutrient content of sprouts actually continues to increase after they've been picked. While very low in calories, sprouts are dense in fiber, vitamins C and A, the minerals iron and folate, and phytochemicals known as glucosinolates, especially sulforaphane, a major inducer of anti-carcinogenic enzymes in the body.

Sprouts add wonderful taste and texture to salads, sandwiches and soups. Try a variety of sprouts, including alfalfa, sunflower, soy, lentil, clover, radish and even grain and nut varieties.

It's important to choose well when deciding which seed companies to try. Be sure to look for organic, non-GMO, non-hybrid, and heirloom seeds. I can't stress those qualities enough.

Health Reasons to Eat Sprouts

- Experts estimate that there can be up to 100 times more enzymes in sprouts than uncooked fruits and vegetables. Enzymes are special types of proteins that act as catalysts for all your body's functions. Extracting more vitamins, minerals, amino acids, and essential fatty acids from the foods you eat ensures that your body has the nutritional building blocks of life to ensure every process works more effectively.

- When you say protein, the first things on people's minds are meat, chicken, fish, egg, and dairy products. What most people do not know is that sprouts are also very high in protein. In fact, they can contain up to 35 percent protein. Adding sprouts to your diet will give you the necessary protein intake required by your body minus the fat, cholesterol, and calories that typically come with animal meats. Sprouts are also highly recommended for vegans and vegetarians.

- The quality and fiber of the protein in the beans, nuts, seeds, or grains improves when it is sprouted. Proteins change during the soaking and sprouting process, improving its nutritional value. The amino acid lysine, for example, which is needed to prevent cold sores and to maintain a healthy immune system increases significantly during the sprouting process. The fiber not only binds to fats and toxins in our body to escort them out, it ensures that any fat our body breaks down is moved quickly out of the body before it can reabsorb through the walls of the intestines.

- Since sprouts are also high in fiber and low in calorie, they can contribute positively to any weight loss diet plan. Eating sprouts will let you enjoy nutrients without the extra calories. It will also make you feel fuller and stave off hunger longer. If you are looking for a way to lose weight, include sprouts in your diet.

- Vitamin content increases dramatically. This is especially true of vitamins A, B-complex, C, and E. The vitamin content of some seeds, grains, beans, or nuts increases by up to 20 times the original value within only a few days of sprouting. Research shows that during the sprouting process mung bean sprouts (or just bean sprouts, as they are often called) increase in vitamin B1 by up to 285 percent, vitamin B2 by up to 515 percent, and niacin by up to 256 percent.

- Essential fatty acid content increases during the sprouting process. Most of us are deficient in these fat-burning essential fats because they are not common in our diet. Eating more sprouts is an excellent way to get more of these important nutrients.

- During sprouting, minerals bind to protein in the seed, grain, nut, or bean, making them more useable in the body. This is true of alkaline minerals like calcium, magnesium, and others that help us to balance our body chemistry for weight loss and better health. Their digestibility is rooted from the high amount of enzymes they contain. Eating sprouts can be very helpful for people with digestive or bloating problems. They are also perfect for younger kids and elderly people.

- Sprouts actually contain oxygen and regular consumption of raw bio-genic foods with their abundant oxygen is valuable to health. Bio-genic foods are a good source of essential fatty acids (the average western diet is generally deficient in these) which play a major role in the immune system defenses.

- Sprouts are the ultimate locally-grown food. When you grow them yourself you are helping the environment and ensuring that you are not getting unwanted pesticides, food additives, and other harmful fat-bolstering chemicals that thwart your weight loss efforts.

- The energy contained in the seed, grain, nut, or legume is ignited through soaking and sprouting.

- Sprouts are alkalizing to your body. Many illnesses including cancer have been linked to excess acidity in the body. Growth of cancer cells are initiated by a lack of oxygen and these cells, along with viruses and bacteria, cannot live in an alkaline and oxygen rich environment. Broccoli sprouts are especially effective at preventing gastritis, ulcers, stomach cancer and even allergy and asthma.

- Sprouts are inexpensive. People frequently use the cost of healthy foods as an excuse for not eating healthy. But, with sprouts being so cheap, there really is no excuse for not eating healthier.

Self-Reliance With Sprouts

Sprouts can be taken camping, hiking and on road trips. You can sprout as you go and have fresh greens everyday.

Besides the fact that sprouts are healthy for everyday eating and should be added to your diet for nutritional reasons, sprouting is an excellent emergency preparedness skill to have. Sprouts provide fresh greens and protein.

From a preparedness standpoint sprouting seeds are a perfect prep: they are compact, they are fast growing, they can easily be germinated indoors, and all you need to activate germination is water. They are also less of a security risk than other food preps, because let's face it, most thieves that would run across seeds wouldn't know what to do with them.

Reasons Sprouts Should Be in Your Food Storage

Nutrition

- Certain seed mixes combine not only for great taste, but for high nutrition. Some seeds provide every amino acid, a long list of vitamins and minerals, and many are high in protein. Access to a fresh, non-meat/dairy source of protein during hard times is highly desirable. Broccoli sprouts are one of the most nutritious, eating one ounce of broccoli sprouts gives you as many antioxidants as 3 pounds of mature broccoli.

Enzymes

- Sprouts are living foods packed with living enzymes ready to take food to its next level. In fact, alfalfa sprouts are one of the healthiest foods available to man with such vital nutrients as calcium, copper, folate, iron, magnesium, manganese, phosphorus, potassium silicon, zinc, Vitamins B, C, D, E and K. Not only do sprouts possess all these nutrients, they're alive and full of enzymes! By the simple application of sprouts in your long-term food storage, you too can enjoy the fresh crisp flavor of vegetables, employing every nutrient for the health of your body from otherwise, "dead" food.

Garden Indoors All Year

- If you live in an extreme climates that limit your outside growing months, you can grow a variety of fresh greens year around. No dirt under the nails, no back breaking work, no worries about early frost.
- If you have a reason for not gardening outside, you can still have fresh greens by sprouting indoors. Sprouts do not need any light for growth. Exposure to sunlight at the end of growing will activate the chlorophyll and green up the sprouts, but it is not a requirement for taste or nutrition.

Portability

- You can sprout on the go by taking your sprouter in the car or even by putting it inside a backpack. In a bug-out situation, you can carry a great deal of food in very little space.

Shelf Life and Compact Storage

- Sprouting seeds have a shelf life of 1 to 5 years depending on the variety. Refrigerating can double the lifespan while freezing can extend it 4 to 5 times. Most sprouting seeds are very small, but grow exponentially.
- The seeds not only store well, but a little goes a long way. In fact, just one pound of alfalfa seeds can produce about ten to fourteen pounds of tasty, fresh sprouts.

The only potential "downside" with sprouting during emergency situations is the amount of water needed. Sprouts need to be initially soaked and then rinsed twice a day. If access to safe water is an issue, it could be difficult to impossible to grow the sprouts. However, sprout water does not need to be discarded. In fact, the water used for the initial soak is full of nutrients that could be consumed as is, used as soup stock, or as needed to reconstitute dehydrated or freeze dried foods.

How to Sprout

Different people will swear by different methods, but I use the most simple and straightforward approach, and I've always been successful.

- Before seeds will sprout, they need to soak. Place the seeds (nuts, grains, legumes) in a bowl and cover with lukewarm water. Soak times vary by species, but a good general guideline is 6-8 hours. It may be shorter for smaller seeds (like sesame and flax) and longer for harder ones (like rye, rice, or lentils).
- Like soak times, sprout times will vary by species. You should continue rinsing your seeds very carefully each day, until they begin to grow their tail. If you want a long

tail, just continue to let them be. But if you want to extend their life, you can refrigerate them to slow the growth. Either way, once the tail is sprouted they are ready to eat. The longer you wait, the more 'watery' and less flavorful they will be (in some cases, this is a good thing). Sprouts will keep for up to 5 days in the fridge.

- After seeds have soaked, remove them from their bath and gently rinse them in a colander or bowl. Place rinsed seeds in a dish or jar, and leave them be, uncovered. Most seeds sprout in 1-3 days.

- Once your beans have sprouted, you can add them to all sorts of culinary creations. There are dozens and dozens of seeds, bean, lentils and nuts you can sprout on their own, but mixing them together is a gourmet treat.

Note:

It's surprising how quickly sprouts can begin to go bad, so it is best to make relatively small amounts of sprouts so they can be eaten within just a couple of days.

If you have sprouts that haven't been eaten for a few days, to keep them from spoiling, it is best to cook them by adding them to a dish you are cooking like curry, stir fry, spaghetti sauce, soup etc.

Sprout Recipes

Why Sprout Chickpeas?

Sprouting chickpeas, (or any bean, grain, seed, and/or nut) is a fabulous idea. Legumes and grains have anti-nutrients inside of them which help protect them in nature but also make them difficult to digest. The process of sprouting neutralizes the anti-nutrients and also unleashes Vitamins and minerals that are trapped inside of the food.

You can add any type of sprouted beans and legumes to any salad (both green and grain salads), Buddha bowl, or even soups.

Sprouted Cooked Hummus

Chickpeas need to be rinsed and soaked in warm water for 24 hours and then let sprout on the counter for 3-5 days.

Soaking chickpeas and preparing them for cooking couldn't be any easier:

- Place 1 cup dried chickpeas in a medium size bowl or jar with enough warm water to cover the beans.
- Stir in 2 tablespoons lemon juice and 1 teaspoon sea salt.
- Cover and let soak up to 24 hours. Chickpeas will double in size.

To sprout chickpeas:

- Rinse the soaked beans and transfer to a large mason jar.
- Cover the jar mouth with a coffee filter secured with a rubber band.
- Place the jar at a 45 degree angle upside down in a clean bowl or pan and let beans sprout for 2-3 days. Rinse a few times each day until sprouts start showing.
- Once the beans are sprouted, rinse them and cook on the stovetop until soft, about an hour.
- Sprouted beans cook faster than only soaked beans.
- Now you have chickpeas that are ready for hummus!

Ingredients:

- 2 cups cooked chickpeas soaked and sprouted
- 1 clove garlic
- 1 lemon juiced

- 1 teaspoon sea salt fine
- 1/4 teaspoon pepper flakes
- 1/4 teaspoon ground cumin
- 2 tablespoons tahini gluten-free
- 1/2 cup olive oil
- 1 tablespoon filtered water optional
- fresh thyme for garnish
- whole chickpeas for garnish

Instructions:

- In a food processor, puree chickpeas and garlic. Then add salt, pepper flakes, cumin, tahini and the juice of one lemon. Keep the food processor running while slowly feeding the olive oil though the tube. Process on and off, scraping the sides of the bowl, until the hummus is smooth and creamy.
- If needed, add one tablespoon of water at the end to cream the hummus even more. Serve right away or store in the refrigerator.

Recipe Notes:

The time needed for this recipe includes only the active prep and cooking time. To soak and sprout chickpeas, please plan ahead and allow three days for soaking and sprouting.

Sprouted Raw Hummus I

You can use this recipe or your own favorite hummus recipe substituting cooked chickpeas with raw sprouted chickpeas. It tastes fresher and creamier than cooked chickpeas.

Ingredients:

- 3/4 cups dried chickpeas
- 1/3 cup tahini
- 1/4 cup lemon juice
- 3 tbsp extra-virgin olive oil
- 2 tbsp apple cider vinegar
- 2 large garlic cloves
- 1/2 tsp salt, I use Himalayan salt
- 1 tsp ground cumin
- ¼ tsp. smoked paprika, optional
- Water, as and if necessary

(Because everyone has different tastes, you will probably want to tweak the amount of lemon juice, tahini, salt and garlic to suit your palate.)

Instructions:

- Start by sprouting the dried chickpeas; this will take about 3 to 5 days, depending on how long you want those sprouts to be.
- When your chickpeas are where you want them, give them a final rinse, drain well, then place them in the container of a high speed blender or food processor, along with the tahini, lemon juice, olive oil, apple cider vinegar, garlic, salt, ground cumin and smoked paprika.
- Process until reduced to a smooth, thick puree, using the tamper if necessary to push the ingredients into the blades and stop the motor to scrape the sides, as needed.
- If you find that your hummus is too thick, you can always add water, a little bit at a time, until you get the desired texture. At this point, you want your hummus to be a little bit thinner than the actual desired texture, as hummus

tends to firm up after a little while (especially if you don't eat it right away and refrigerate it).

- Serve immediately with fresh crudités, tortillas, pita bread, or use in your favorite sandwich or recipe. Or, just plain grab a spoon and dig in!
- Leftovers will keep in an airtight container for up to 5 days

Hummus Sandwiches:

Toast 6 to 8 slices of Goddess Sourdough Bread and spread desired amount of hummus over each piece. Layer the greens, avocado, red onion, and tomato, and top with the remaining slices. Cut sandwiches in half, serve, and enjoy!

Sprouted Hummus II

Ingredients:

1 cup of sprouted garbanzo beans
1 Tbs. tahini
1 Tbs. lemon juice
1 Tsp. olive oil
1 clove garlic (more or less - to taste)
1 tsp. ground cumin
1/2 tsp. salt
1/2 tsp. ground white pepper
Hot Sauce of your choosing (optional)

Directions:

Mix all ingredients to desired consistency using a food processor. For creamier hummus use hot water or more tahini.

Avocado-Sprout Toast

A fresh take on the classic flavors of smashed avocado on toast. Add a sprinkle of nutrient-rich sunflower seeds for extra crunch.

Ingredients:

1 slice whole-grain long ferment sourdough bread, toasted
1/2 ripe avocado, sliced
Dash of sea salt
Dash of black pepper
1/4 cup alfalfa sprouts, or any sprouts you like
2 teaspoons sunflower seeds
1/2 teaspoon fresh lemon juice, squeezed over the top

Strawberry Smoothie

Ingredients:

- 1 1/2 cup frozen strawberries (use 3/4 cup of ice if fresh berries are used)
- 1 cup any milk
- 1 tsp. vanilla
- 1/4 cup any leafy sprouts
- 1 Tbs. chia seeds (you can soak these for 20 minutes in water before using them if you want. They will be thicker if you do.
- 1 Tbs. honey or other sweetener, if desired.

Directions:

- Place all ingredients in blender and blend until smooth.

- Add frozen banana pieces for a strawberry-banana smoothie.

Herb Sprouts

Ingredients:

- 1 - 5 cups of sprouts, depending on your taste
- (Mixed sprouts and Almonds is an excellent combination, also any bean sprouts you like will be wonderful)
- 1 tbs. ground oregano
- 1 tbs. ground basil
- 1 tbs. ground thyme
- 1 tsp. pepper
- 1 tsp. garlic powder
- 1 tsp. onion powder
- 1 tsp. ground rosemary
- 1 tsp. ground marjoram
- 1 tsp. olive oil per pound of sprouts

Directions:

- Mix all ingredients together.
- Sprinkle Parmesan cheese on top.

Microgreens

Microgreens are sprouting up everywhere from upscale restaurants to home gardens. They help spruce up old recipes with intense flavors and colors, and are packed with nutrients.

Microgreens are typically seedlings of spinach, lettuce, red cabbage and other veggies that are usually 1-3 inches in height and harvested within 14 days of germination. They enhance the color, texture and flavor of salads, soups, sandwiches and other foods.

Organic Popcorn Shoots

Popcorn shoots are quite tasty! They're a bit sweet and have a very subtle taste of sweet corn.

You will need:

- a recycled plastic salad container
- potting soil
- organic popcorn

Directions:

Fill container with about two inches tall of potting soil. Make certain that the container has drainable holes to allow excess water to escape. Scatter popcorn over the soil. In this case, don't worry about overcrowding the seeds – the wee corn sprouts don't mind being crowded. You want the seeds to be in a pretty solid single layer on top of the soil.

Cover popcorn with a layer of potting soil about one inch thick. Water thoroughly and close the plastic lid. This helps to retain moisture until the popcorn shoots sprout.

Place in a sunny window, being sure to use a drainage container underneath it to capture moisture. In two or three days you'll see tiny popcorn shoots starting to appear. At this point, you'll want to open the lid to give the growing corn sprouts room to grow. Watch the growing popcorn shoots carefully and water as needed to keep the soil damp but not overly wet.

In another couple of days, the popcorn sprouts will be 2 inches tall and ready to harvest. Don't let them get much taller than that, or they'll lose their sweetness.

To harvest, simply use scissors to snip them off at the base. And surprise! Those seeds will push out a second harvest in another couple of days. Use these popcorn shoots as you would any other microgreen: Add to salads, sandwiches, and wraps or just snack on them plain.

CHAPTER 16

Fermented Food

Dramatically improve your health by eating foods filled with dynamic probiotics that supercharge your body! Ordinary foods become powerful health agents in a few easy steps using ancient wisdom and time-tested techniques such as natural fermentation. This is information that has not been publicized much but is very important for your health.

Humans have dried, salted and fermented foods since before recorded history. Preserving food by heat-treating and then sealing it in airtight containers didn't come along until the late 18th century.

Before there was modern day canning, people needed a way to preserve their food to last longer and lacto fermentation does just that. Almost every traditional culture has fermented some sort of food to prevent spoilage. A honey wine, called mead, is thought to be one of the most ancient preserved foods, dating back thousands of years.

The act of traditionally preparing food unlocks nutrients, enhances digestion, encourages healthy gut flora, and much more. Nutrients in traditionally-prepared foods are more easily assimilated by the body because the nutrients are in a more available state. Any anti-nutrients blocking absorption or inhibiting enzyme function are now neutralized. Traditionally prepared foods are things like lacto-fermentation, sourdough and cultured dairy.

Weston A. Price, a dentist who traveled the world, studying primitive cultures found that almost all of the traditional cultures had some form of lacto-fermentation as part of their food culture. Many fermented foods were made from dairy products. Nomadic herders found that raw, unpasteurized milk would quickly ferment causing the milk to separate (curds from the whey) and would become a more stable and storable dairy product.

Lacto fermented; Despite the word 'lacto' most of the ferments are dairy-free. These lacto fermented foods refer to the 'lactobacilli', not lactose. Lactobacilli bacteria give us the probiotics we need for healthy digestion. These microorganisms also preserve our food, allowing tomatoes picked at the peak of ripeness in August to be turned into delicious homemade salsa used all winter!

Lacto fermentation is the process of beneficial bacteria that are naturally occurring on vegetables and converting them to lactic acid. Not only is lacto fermented foods delicious but they are also rich in probiotics. Lacto-fermentation not only helps preserve food, but it also increases the vitamin and enzyme levels, as well as helps the digestibility of the fermented food. Eating fermented foods like pickles or carrots are a great way to add gut-healthy probiotics to your diet. It's basically like taking probiotic pills.

Foods that were once traditionally fermented or cultured, are now preserved in different ways (pickling with vinegar and canning for example) so the good bacteria is no longer present. Imagine taking real, whole foods and preparing them as most people do nowadays (quick-yeasted bread, or cooked-to-death veggies canned in white vinegar). It's no wonder many of us suffer from food sensitivities. Our bodies simply can't access the nutrients we're eating.

One of the main benefits healthy gut bacteria has been shown to help your immune system, decrease inflammation, and can help decrease the incidence of certain diseases like heart disease. Studies are finding gut bacteria may cause rheumatoid arthritis.

Fermented vs Pickled

The main difference between pickled and fermented foods is how they're made. Basically, pickled foods are preserved through the acidity, while fermented foods are preserved through the bacteria and the fermentation processes.

Pickling:

With pickling, you're immersing the ingredients in something acidic, like vinegar. The process alters the texture and the taste of food, creating a sour flavor. There are various ways to pickle foods. But, you'll always be using some type of acidic solution. Most pickling approaches rely on heat too. That heat helps destroy any dangerous microbes and helps the food last longer, but it also kills the enzymes and good bacteria.

Pickled food are hardened by the action of acetic acid and sometimes by alcohol. They arrest the action of the saliva and cause catarrh, (a discharge from the mucus membranes). Acetic action is an active poison. Pickles, stuffed olives, brandied fruit, etc. are all in the same class. Salads in which vinegar is used are far from wholesome, cause great irritation and must be eliminated from the diet of the sick and invalid.

Fermentation:

Fermenting doesn't involve any extra acid. Instead, the sour taste comes from the reaction between compounds in the food and bacteria that are naturally present. Humans have always enjoyed the distinctive flavors of tangy sauerkraut, earthy miso and sublime wines.

When you consume a fermented food, you're eating the transformed food, along with the colonies of bacteria. The process doesn't sound appealing, but fermented foods are safe and should be a common part of our diets. Plus, the bacteria are all good for you. They can help support the healthy bacteria that live in your gut. Integrating more plant foods and fermented foods like kimchi and kombucha can make a huge difference in changing your internal biome in weeks, not years.

There is so many ways to enjoy ferments. All you need is a little creativity. It really is a glorious and delicious way to eat your harvest, stay healthy and build up your food storage.

- Sparkling Beverages
- Sourdough Bread
- Cheese
- Sauerkraut, chutney, pickles and relish
- Beer, wine, cider and mead
- Kombucha
- Kefir
- Miso
- Tempeh
- Kimchi

Overall, fermented foods are much more relevant for health than pickled foods. Fermented foods should be a part of your diet for this reason alone. Adding fermented foods to your diet is easy and, if you make them yourself, very affordable. A serving of cultured food can contain 10s of trillions of probiotics. That is equal to an entire jar of an expensive over the counter probiotic capsules.

For beginners, fermentation might seem a little daunting, however. It's definitely a learning process, but thankfully it's not hard at all. I recommend beginning by reading some great books on fermentation, there are recommendations is the reference section.

Fermented foods are also becoming easier to find as their popularity increases. You'll often find products like these at grocery stores and health food stores. Some cafés and restaurants are even beginning to offer fermented foods. So, even if you don't want to do fermentation yourself, there are plenty of options for eating fermented foods regularly.

Recipes

Probiotic-Rich Fermented Cinnamon Apples

These Probiotic-Rich Fermented Cinnamon Apples taste like apple pie but they are so healthy! This is the perfect recipe for those who are interested in fermented foods because the recipe is simple and the flavor is great.

Ingredients:

- 1 tsp Himalayan salt or Celtic sea salt
- 1 TBSP ground cinnamon
- Juice from one real lemon (not from concentrate)
- 2 TBSP fermented tea from a SCOBY (kombucha) OR use 1/2 tsp of Culture Starter
- 3-4 cups chopped organic sweet apples (ex: Honeycrisp)
- Water, filtered

Instructions:

- Mix salt, cinnamon, lemon juice, and starter culture in a medium-sized mixing bowl
- Cut the apples into quarters, remove seeds, and chop. Toss the chopped apples in the ingredients in the mixing bowl.
- Pack the apples and ingredients from your mixing bowl into your canning jars. Fill with water covering the apples but leaving about an inch of space left at the top for expansion.
- Put the lids on and store at room temperature out of direct sunlight for 48 hours.

Place the jars in the refrigerator after 2 days if you are not consuming the apples right away. Keep refrigerated for up to 3 months.

Fermented Carrots

Ingredients:

- 1 pound whole carrots
- 4 tablespoons sea salt

Optional Added Ingredients:

- 1" chunk of fresh ginger, peel the ginger and slice into discs or chunks
- 1/2 tsp turmeric powder

Instructions:

- Bring 2 cups of water to a light simmer. Remove it from the heat and stir in the salt, until dissolved.
- Add the salt water to a half gallon glass mason jar. Fill the jar the rest of the way with filtered water.
- Slice the carrots into long thin sticks. Put them in another half gallon mason jar, and pour the prepared brine over them until they are fully submerged. Leave one to two inches headspace.
- Add some kind of fermenting weight to keep the carrots underneath the liquid. This could be a folded up cabbage leaf or a rock in a ziplock bag. If you plan to ferment often, you could even buy weights specifically made for fermenting. To successfully lacto-ferment anything, the veggies have to be submerged under the brine completely.
- Cover with a loose lid, or a tea towel and rubber band.
- Allow the carrots to sit in an undisturbed place for 2-14 days. Over the first few days you will see little activity, then on day 3-4 you may see small bubbles (fermenting activity). The amount of time will depend on the temperature in the house and your preferences. You can give the veggies a little taste each day to see if the desired taste and texture is reached.

- Once the carrots are done fermenting, cover them with a tight lid and move the jar to the refrigerator.
- When they are done fermenting, take it easy opening the jar as pressure builds up from the ferment and you may have some spillage. I would open it over the sink just to eliminate the chance for messes.

Fermented Grapefruit Juice

Ingredients:

- 2 1/2 cups fresh squeezed grapefruit juice
- 1 cup filtered water
- 1/2 tsp culture starter or 2 tbsp whey
- pinch sea salt

Instructions:

- Pour juice and water into quart size mason jar
- Add culture starter or whey
- Add pinch of salt
- Cover tightly, give a quick shake to mix and leave at room temperature for 24-48 hours.

Refrigerate and enjoy!

Be sure to open carefully as gases do build up during fermentation.

Preserved/Fermented Lemons

Ingredients:

- 5-6 Lemons (organic is best because of pesticides), reserve ½ of one lemon
- 3 Tablespoons of Real Salt
- 1 quart Mason Jar

- Water, filtered

Instruction:

- Gather those gorgeous lemons and a sharp knife.
- Cut the end off of each lemon.
- Cut each lemon in half. Set aside ½ of a lemon- uncut. You will be reserving this ½ for juicing.
- Quarter each lemon.
- Take each quarter and slice them into ½ inch (or so) slices.
- Pack sliced lemons into mason jar.
- Make your brine. Add 3 Tablespoons of salt to 1 quart of warm (not hot) water. (Note: you will not use all of this brine, but I would rather have too much than not enough. I store the extra brine in the fridge until I can use it again. You can use it for pasta water, fermenting other foods, etc.).
- Pour brine into jar packed with those gorgeous lemons. Squeeze the juice from the ½ of a lemon that is set aside into the jar.
- Add your weight to keep lemons below the brine.
- Cover with a regular lid and band. You will have to remember to "burp" the jar every day.
- Place the lemons in a cool/dark place for 2-4 weeks. After that, transfer to the top shelf of your fridge or a root cellar.

Notes:

Lemons will keep for 6-12 months in the fridge/root cellar, although they probably won't last that long.

Use the lemons as you would a normal lemon. You can also use the lemon juice brine. Taste them before using. If they seem salty just use less salt in what you are cooking.

The recipes above are just a sampling of foods you can ferment. There are many books and recipes online.

CHAPTER 17

Dehydrating Food

One of the best methods for preserving food is drying or dehydrating. It preserves food by simply removing the water. Bacteria, mold, and yeasts cannot grow in dry environments. It's probably the oldest method of preserving food, but in the past, it wasn't used by people living in humid areas. High humidity can prevent food from drying properly without smoking it or using some of today's handy technology. Thankfully, there are now many methods to dehydrate food right in your home. Some are cheaper and more efficient than others, but no matter how you dehydrate food, there are a ton of benefits.

If you use a low enough temperature when drying, the foods' naturally present nutrition remains. Specifically, vitamins and enzymes. This is not the case with high-heat canning or higher-heat dehydrating. Vegetables, fruits, herbs, eggs, dairy, meats, you name it, can be saved beyond their season through drying.

Everyone is facing changing times politically, economically, and environmentally. In a world with little certainty, you want to be prepared in whatever way you can. Whether there's a natural disaster or you lose your job, having food on hand can make your life much easier when things get tough.

Dehydrating food can quickly and cheaply provide you with a lot of stored food. Dried food will last about a year in sealed bags or containers and will last indefinitely if you vacuum seal it.

It's perfect for camping trips and survival situations. Unlike frozen food, it doesn't require a constant energy source to keep from spoiling. You can take it anywhere no matter what the outside temperature is.

Also, because you're taking out all the water when you dehydrate food, it becomes lighter and smaller, especially when compared to canned foods which can be a hassle to transport. This is exactly why nomadic people of the past often dried their food.

Food for Emergencies

Home-dehydrated meals takes up half the space of store-bought freeze-dried meals, so you can carry a week's supply of backpacking food without hiring a goat.

Having this supply of dehydrated meals on hand means your family is always prepared for emergencies. Vacuum seal the meals, so they are safe and delicious to eat whenever you need them.

Space Saving

When you dehydrate the water out of these foods and then store them dried, the space that they will take up ranges from 5-16% of their original size. Think about the difference between storing a teeny tiny bag of sun-dried tomatoes in your fridge versus finding space for 5 quart jars on your shelf. You can also dehydrate frozen vegetables to save space in your freezer.

Benefits Of Dehydrating Food

- **Maintains More Nutrients Than Other Food Preservation Methods**

There are only small amounts of nutrient loss in comparison with other food preservation methods like canning and freezing. Dehydration has a 3-5% nutrient loss after preservation. Freezing has a 40 – 60% nutrient loss and canning has 60-80% nutrient loss.

You can still technically have raw food if you keep the heat under 115 degrees while dehydrating.

- **Minimal Work Involved**

Dehydrated foods often require very minimal preparation prior to dehydration. Most of the time, you cut the food to the desired size, blanch (if needed) and place on the trays and then dehydrate. Dehydration is so great for when you don't have all night to spend canning a garden harvest.

- **Food Stays Fresh without Power**

If your electricity ever goes out, dehydrated food is safe. After a week at room temperature, just about everything in the refrigerator and freezer will be rotten.

Having dehydrated food eliminates the risk of loss. You also don't need to pay to keep it frozen. For an electric dehydrator you use the initial power and that's it. If you have a solar dehydrator you use no electricity and it costs you nothing!

- **Long Shelf Life**

In general, dried fruits and vegetables are expected to last about 5 years under optimal conditions. That's 3 Years longer than canned goods and 4 years longer than frozen food.

- **More Food in a Small Area**

Massive amount of food shrinks down so small! Different fruits and vegetables shrink different amounts based on how much water content they have.

This helps cut down the space needed for food storage. It also allows you to take more food with you if you should have to leave your home in an emergency.

- **Saves Money**

A dehydrator can save you tons of money in multiple ways. One way is that you save the garden bounty to use later. Not sure what to do with all those extra peppers or jalapenos? Dehydrate them. Can't figure out how to use the millions of zucchini coming off your plants? Dehydrate them!

When winter comes and you need jalapenos for your chili or zucchini for a vegetable or minestrone soup just throw them in and let them simmer and re-hydrate. It's so easy!

The beautiful benefit of this is you don't end up going to the store to buy those things "fresh" (really in the middle of winter they are coming from 1000+ miles away in Mexico if you live in the U.S. To me that's anything but fresh). You save that money and you have garden bounty right in the middle of winter.

- **It's Foolproof**

Its really hard to over dry a food because of the low temperatures used to dehydrate. If you ever leave a dehydrated food out for a bit and it partially re-hydrates, all you have to do is throw it back in the dehydrator and it's good to go!

- **Portable**

Dehydrated food is so lightweight it's easy to tote anywhere without the added weight! It can be carried around without the need of refrigeration or ice packs to keep it cool.

- **Intense Flavor**

Removing all the water from the food leaves you with some wonderful intense flavors. My favorites foods that get more intense flavors with dehydrating are kale and strawberries.

- **Rehydrate**

To rehydrate foods, plan to place 1 cup of food in 1 cup of hot or cool water, depending on your planned use. Once this is completed, allow up to four hours for rehydration. Use as you would normally in your recipe.

Methods of Food Dehydrating

There are a few ways to go about dehydrating your food, but some methods are more successful than others. That's because modern tools have helped improve the rate of dehydration, reducing the chance your food will spoil. Here are the most common methods used today.

Sun Drying

It's hard to think of an older or simpler way to preserve food than sun drying. For about 12,000 years people have sliced fruit and placed it on racks or lines in the sunshine. Sun drying is very effective in places with long periods of hot sun. The ancient Romans commonly ate raisins and dried figs thanks to their Mediterranean climate. But anywhere with a minimum temperature of 86 F and a relative humidity of 60% will work. Just remember that fruit takes several days to dry thoroughly. Place on a mesh screen (avoiding anything galvanized) and cover with a second screen to deter flies and other insects.

Air Drying

Like sun drying, air drying is an ancient method of dehydrating food. The main difference is that air drying usually takes place in the shade. That's because this method helps preserves anything that needs protection from the sun's rays. It works well for delicate greens and herbs, especially those you're saving for culinary mixes or herbal teas.

Solar Drying

A step up from sun drying, solar drying uses a dehydrator powered by the sun to passively dry your food. Since there's no element to provide heat or fans to circulate the air, solar drying uses no electricity. Solar dryers work outdoors and are usually designed like a mini tabletop greenhouse.

Oven Drying

Oven drying uses your home oven to slowly dry food at temperatures around 140 F. Because ovens are so large, they're not the most efficient dryers on the block. But they can save you the trouble of buying an extra appliance if quick drying is your goal. They can also warm up your house, since you'll need to prop the door open to let the moisture escape. If you're thinking of drying food in your oven, check to make sure your oven goes low enough. Anything over 140 F will cook your food instead of drying it.

Electric Dehydrating

Add modern technology to age-old drying techniques and presto: you have electric dehydrators. These little powerhouses come equipped with fans and elements to quickly and efficiently dry your food. That means virtually no spoilage and a tasty end result. Most electric dehydrators also come with a temperature gauge and adjustment dial. This helps to speed or slow drying time depending on what you're processing.

If your food dehydrator does have a fan, consider using it in your garage or another area where noise won't matter. This advice also applies if you're using your food dehydrator in summer and you don't want to heat up your living space.

What Can You Dehydrate?

You can dehydrate almost any fresh food, but some things dehydrate better than others. Here are some favorites.

- Fruits (apples, bananas, apricots, peaches, pears, cherries, blueberries) for eating as snacks or chopped in granola and trail mixes, or dried as purees for fruit leather.
- Vegetables (carrots, mushrooms, onions, peas, beans, tomatoes) for adding to soups, stews, and backpacking meals.
- Meat and fish (ground beef, chicken, or turkey; sliced meats; cured meats; fresh fish; beef jerky) for adding to backpacking meals or storing for soup and stew ingredients.

- Nuts, seeds (walnuts, hazelnuts, almonds, pecans, macadamia) after soaking or sprouting, to make them more digestible.
- Sprouted grains (rice, buckwheat, barley, quinoa, amaranth) to preserve nutrients and to store for flours, granolas, and baking.
- Herbs (oregano, basil, parsley, dill, fennel, mint, lemon balm, hyssop) for later use in teas, baking, and cooking.
- Crackers, breads, and granolas for raw food diets.

To Blanch or Not To Blanch

Blanching refers to pre-heating your vegetables, fruits, and meats before placing them in your dehydrator. People usually blanch vegetables, particularly those that take longer to cook, because it helps prevent flavor loss before drying. The easiest way to blanch is to place vegetables in the basket of your steamer and heat water beneath. Steam for 2 to 5 minutes until vegetables are heated to the center.

The most common vegetables to blanch include:

- Asparagus (3 to 5 minutes)
- Broccoli (3 to 5 minutes)
- Cabbage (2 to 3 minutes)
- Carrots (3 to 4 minutes)
- Corn (1 to 3 minutes)
- Green beans (4 to 5 minutes)
- Peas (3 minutes)
- Kale, spinach (just until wilted)

How To Dehydrate Food

Dehydrating food takes a lot of time, but not time that you have to directly put in. Once your food is processed and in the dehydrator, you can walk away for hours. For example, if you want to preserve apples, you can cut them up and toss them in the dehydrator.

For home food drying, you will need:

- Dehydrator or Drying Rack
- Sharp knife and cutting board
- Large, heavy duty pot
- Blender or food processor (for "leathers")
- Salad spinner (optional)
- Specialty items such as cherry pitters and apples corers speed up processing, if you dehydrate a lot of those fruits.
- A mandolin slicer will help with uniform thickness and drying time

You may choose to use an electric dehydrator, but during the summer months when most produce is available anyway, solar dehydrators are a great option. Using a solar dehydrator is one of the only methods of food preservation that can be done without any energy.

Commercial dehydrators give more consistent results and are easier to work with, giving you a better quality end product. Quick and uniform drying preserves color, flavor and texture. Most commercial units also allow you to set your temperature, which is very helpful for optimal drying of different foods. For instance, herbs dry best at lower temperatures so that you don't drive off volatile oils, while meats are typically dried at higher temps.

Making your own dehydrated food, particularly fruits, is a great way to make the most of fresh foods when they are in season and inexpensive. For example, tomatoes can vary as much as 500% over the year as they go from feast to famine. By dehydrating your own foods you know exactly what has or hasn't been added to the mix, making them healthier snacks for the whole family.

CHAPTER 18

What About Bread?

You can't fix your health until you fix your diet.
When it comes to bread you either have
to eat the proper bread or eliminate it .

Bread, in one form or another, has been one of the principal life sustaining forms of food for man from earliest times.

Whole grain, water and salt. These basic ingredients have fed humanity for millennia. Combined in innumerable ways, they form bread. As a basic food, bread has everything necessary to sustain life, which is miraculous given the simplicity of its elements. For the majority of ancient people, bread was the centerpiece of most meals. The classic texts of antiquity detail its prevalence and use. Enjoyed alongside sumptuous feasts or the sole item for a meal, the baking and eating of bread has been a food tradition regardless of economic class or status.

In the Stone Age, people made solid cakes from stone-crushed barley and wheat. A millstone used for grinding corn has been found, that is thought to be 7,500 years old. The ability to sow and reap cereals may be one of the chief causes which led the ancients to dwell in communities, rather than to live a wandering life hunting and gathering.

According to botanists, wheat, oats, barley and other grains belong to the order of Grasses; nobody has yet found the wild form of grass from which wheat, as we know it, has developed. Like most of the wild grasses, cereal blossoms bear both male and female elements. The young plants are provided with a store of food to ensure their support during the period of germination, and it is in this store of reserve substance that the ancients found an abundant supply of food.

It could be said when ancient humans discovered a food which would keep through the winter months, and could be multiplied in the summer, is when civilization began. They might have had a reasonably safe store of food to carry them over, which would give them time to develop other useful skills.

In Old Testament times, all the evidence points to the fact that bread-making, preparing the grain, making the bread and baking it, was the women's work, but in the palaces of kings and princes and in large households, the bakers' duties would be specialized. Bread was leavened, that is, an agent in the form of a 'barm' was added to the dough which caused the mixture to rise in the shape of our familiar loaf. The hurried departure of the Israelites from Egypt, described in the Book of Exodus in the Bible, prevented their bread being leavened as usual; the Jews today commemorate this event by eating unleavened bread on special occasions. The ruins of Pompeii and other buried cities have revealed the kind of bakeries existing in those historic times. There were public bakeries where the poorer people brought their bread to be baked, or from which they could buy ready-baked bread.

The trade of the baker is one of the oldest crafts in the world. Loaves and rolls have been found in ancient Egyptian tombs. In the British Museum's Egyptian galleries you can see actual loaves which were made and baked over 5,000 years ago. Also on display are grains of wheat which ripened in those ancient summers under the Pharaohs. Wheat has been found in pits where human settlements flourished 8,000 years ago.

The stone-age method of pounding wheat between two stones was not basically very different from the method of grinding by millstones in a wind or watermill. In either case the bottom stone was fixed, and a grinding movement by the top stone was the required action to produce ground meal. The stones were round, the bottom one fixed and the top stone, or runner, was balanced on a spindle which could be raised or lowered, making the space between it and the bottom stone as narrow or as wide as the miller wanted. Both stones were corrugated, so that when the top stone was running, the wheat between it and the bed was scraped rather than bruised. The wheat to be ground entered the mill by a hole in the top stone, and was carried out towards the edge, leaving in the form of a meal by holes round the outside of the bed. By raising or lowering the top stone, the meal could be made as fine or as coarse as required.

In today's modern mills the whole process of cleaning, and milling, etc., is done by machine, with the material passing automatically from machine to machine, and from one stage to the next. No hand touches the wheat from the moment it arrives, throughout its long journey in the mill, until the flour leaves the mill for the baker, cereal and biscuit-makers and other users.

Bread has been the most important item in our diet for millennia; it has often been called the staff of life for good reason. To give you an idea of the benefit we get from whole grain flour and bread, a Government survey showed that flour and bread provided us with more energy value, more protein, more iron, more nicotinic acid and more vitamin B1 than any other basic food. One could live very well on a diet of only whole wheat bread, whole rye bread or whole barley bread, with vegetables and fruit added.

Whole wheat flour is rich in carbohydrates (for energy), protein (for growth and development), the essential B vitamins (for good health, good nerves and good digestion) and important minerals like iron (for healthy blood) and calcium (for strong bones and teeth). If you use 100 percent whole grain bread, you will find it to be a good source of fiber, vitamins, minerals and complex carbohydrates. Bread is low in fat, one slice of bread is about 70 calories.

Why then are so any people getting sick from eating wheat products? It's clear that celiac disease and gluten sensitivity has become much more prevalent over the past 5 to 10 years. Gluten-free food choices are everywhere. So why such a sudden increase? Why didn't our ancestors suffer from the same conditions?

The Health Wrecking Ingredients in Modern Bread

The original bread from the ancients, until about 100 years ago, were 3 ingredients, organic whole grain, pure water and a little salt if they had it. This was the staff of life from the earliest of times but with man's manipulations has become the staff of death. Nature never intended that wheat and other grains be separated into their different parts, presented to the people as a wonderful invention, then sold for a big price. Untold harm is done by the bakery goods on the market today. They are baked just enough to stand up, but not enough to kill the yeast germ or fermented to break down the gluten or change the starch into an easy to digest form.

Bread Available Today On Grocery Store Shelves Can Have 30 + Ingredients

Ingredient list for Wonder Bread:

Wheat Flour Enriched (Flour, Barley Malt, Ferrous Sulfate [Iron], Vitamin B [Niacin Vitamin B3, Thiamine Mononitrate Vitamin B1 {Thiamin Vitamin B1}, Riboflavin Vitamin B2

{Riboflavin Vitamin B2}, Folic Acid Vitamin B9]), Water, Corn Syrup High Fructose, Contains 22% or less, Wheat Gluten, Salt, Soybean Oil, Yeast, Calcium Sulfate, Vinegar, Monoglyceride, Dough Conditioners (Sodium Stearoyl Lactylate, Calcium Dioxide), Soy Flour, Diammonium Phosphate, Dicalcium Phosphate, Monocalcium Phosphate, Yeast Nutrients (Ammonium Sulfate), Calcium Propionate

Dough Conditioners: These are unnecessary in traditional bread making and only make the process faster and cheaper for the food industry to make bread in big machinery. Many dough conditioners like azodicarbonamide (which is banned all over the world), DATEM, monoglycerides, diglycerides, sodium stearoyl lactylate are linked to health issues. Many dough conditioners start with manipulating fat, like soybean oil or corn oil, which is also most likely GMO.

Preservatives: Commercial bread is supposed to be fresh and eaten within a few days from baking unless frozen. You see preservatives like calcium propionate, which is linked to ADHD.

GMOs: Most commercially available breads contain one or many genetically modified ingredients like soy lecithin, soybean oil, corn oil, corn starch or soy flour. You may have heard the argument that genetic modification has been happening since the dawn of time. This argument states that farmers have been cross breeding crops for desired traits since the dawn of time so why is it such a big deal now?

The answer is that we're talking about two completely different processes. Cross breeding between similar species of plants for desirable traits is what has been happening for thousands of years. The genetic modification (aka genetic engineering) happening in the last few decades is taking place in a laboratory at a cellular level. Genes are being manipulated, traded and inserted into crops in a way that could never be produced in nature. GMOs have not been tested long term on humans, however we know that the pesticides sprayed on them are absolutely toxic and considered to be poisonous. Some GMOs are created by inserting a toxic pesticide into the seed itself to make an insect's stomach explode when they try to eat it.

GMO ingredients you will find in a loaf of bread:

One of the major GMO players is soy, as in soy flour, soy lecithin, and soybean oil. Soy lecithin is used for its ability to make bread dough easy to work with by making it less sticky. Soy flour has a bleaching affect on dough and it adds softness and volume to mass produced breads. And Soybean oil is used to extend shelf life, add flavor and make bread softer. Another GMO ingredient to look out for in bread is cornstarch which is sometimes used for its thickening ability and as a component for bleaching flour.

You should also watch out for corn oil, vegetable oil, cottonseed oil, dextrose and high fructose corn syrup as they are likely to be genetically modified. And even trickier are enzymes commonly added to dough to make processing easier or to help create a good crust. Many of them are made with the help of genetically modified microorganisms, not that you can find this anywhere on a label.

GMO ingredients are used in breads for a ton of different reasons, for bread to seem thicker, for dough to be easier to work with, to improve bread coloring, to add nutritional value etc., but the #1 main reason they are used all ties into the fact that most breads are massed produced.

Added Sugar: This is where you really need to watch out. There's nothing wrong with a little honey to bring out the sweetness in whole wheat bread, but most manufactures are using high fructose corn syrup, GMO sugar made from sugar beets, or some other artificial sweetener like "Sucralose" that are not the best forms of sugar and can pose health risks. Almost all commercially baked brands have some form of added sweetener, especially watch out for "light" breads, which often contain more added sugar.

Artificial Flavors and Coloring: These ingredients are made from petroleum and are linked to several health issues like hyperactivity in children, allergies and asthma. They are easy to spot on the label because the FDA requires it. However, ingredients like "caramel coloring" can fool you into thinking this ingredient is a real food. Most industrial caramel coloring is created by heating ammonia and is considered a carcinogen when created this way. Yellow #5 and Yellow #6 are used for caramel coloring.

Synthetic Vitamins: Synthetic vitamins are used in bread to replace the natural ones that are destroyed during the milling and refinement process in most baked goods. The components added back to the flour are actually toxic!

Iron is a "nutrient" added to enriched flour, except the type of iron added is not really a nutrient at all, but is considered a metallic iron. Metallic iron is not bioavailable to the human body and was never meant to be consumed. Enriched flour is not absorbed by the body as wheat or a grain, in which case your body could use the energy slowly and effectively, but as a starch. That is because the wheat germ has been stripped from the flour; the FDA states that enriched flour cannot have more than 5 percent wheat germ.

Pesticides: The wheat that is used to make most bread is heavily sprayed with pesticides. Over the past 15 years, there has also been a dramatic increase in the use of the broad-spectrum herbicide Roundup by farmers. It has become a common harvest protocol to spray wheat fields with Roundup, allowing for an earlier, easier and bigger harvest. This saves money and increases profits.

The research suggests that glyphosate can kill the beneficial bacteria in our gastrointestinal system. This beneficial bacteria, more commonly known as probiotics, plays a key role in digestive health by preventing the permeability of the gastrointestinal tract, synthesizing nutrients, and providing the foundation for robust immunity. By destroying these healthy bacteria, glyphosate can contribute to numerous modern diseases that result from digestive dysfunction, including depression, celiac disease and gluten sensitivity.

In other words, glyphosate reduces the bacteria in our bodies that help us digest food. When the probiotics in our gut get destroyed by glyphosate, genetically-susceptible individuals have a much more difficult time breaking down wheat and absorbing vitamins and minerals, which results in chronic disease. By choosing certified organic products you will avoid exposure to the poison and GMOs.

Bleached White Flour: Wheat has three parts to it: the bran; which is packed with fiber, the endosperm; the largest part of the seed and made up of mostly starch, and the germ; the nutrient-rich embryo of the seed.

The refining process associated with making white flour separates the fiber-rich bran from the rest of the grain, so white flour typically contains less fiber than its whole-grain counterpart.

White flour is really nothing more than refined carbohydrates and can contribute to obesity. Studies show that Americans eat enough extra calories (mostly through refined carbs) to add three pounds of body fat per month to their weight.

Carbs should come from unrefined sources, like fresh organic fruits and vegetables. Not from something that's been processed, bleached, and treated with synthetic nutrients.

Baker's Yeast: Bakers yeast in bread can also aggravate gut-related disorders. Where patients have a history of long courses of antibiotics, which create imbalances in gut bacteria, yeast can flourish. It can cause headaches, aching joints and thrush.

Candida and anemia are related to the consumption of yeasted bread. Rickets and anemia can be caused by the consumption of yeasted whole wheat bread. These chronic calcium deficiencies are corrected and even totally eliminated when the whole wheat bread is naturally leavened. In the natural leavening process, the phytic acid and the phytates are hydrolysed by the phytases of the bran in an acid environment and transformed into phytin and soluble phosphatic acids of magnesium, calcium and iron which are totally assimilable and beneficial.

Vital Wheat Gluten: Something you need to know is that ancient grain flours are notoriously hard to work when baking bread. The chemical makeup of the gluten in ancient grains makes it different from that of modernized wheat(s).

Heirloom Spelt, for instance, does contain gluten but the gluten is very fragile. This makes it great for digestion purposes but hard for bakers to handle and even harder for companies to mass produce without added ingredients.

Vital Wheat Gluten is added to breads and other baked goods because it helps provide the strength and elasticity necessary to endure the often brutal process of commercial mixing. Plus it helps produce a fluffy, light textured loaf of bread and has become somewhat the standard in the baking industry.

Mass Production: Mass producing a bread means there is no room for error. The dough has to be easy to work with. The dough cannot be sticky when making its way through machinery. The bread has to be shelf stable and able to last for weeks after it is purchased. Above all else, it has to be consistent for mass producing to be possible.

With industrialization, came mass-produced food made by machines rather than human hands. "Commercial" yeast was developed to facilitate faced-paced factory production of bread without much input from a human being. Interestingly, one theory as to where the wild yeast comes from in natural leaving is from bakers working the starters with their hands. So maybe the mechanization of the bread baking process necessitated the introduction of yeast from another source, something to replace the yeast that had previously come from the human. When machines began to make bread, the bread lost the flavor, character, and nutritional value that it once had. And bakers became technicians rather than craftspeople.

The popularity of commercial yeast spread to home baking and to most small bakeries. Throughout most of the industrialized world, the craft of bread making as it had been practiced for thousands of years was all but lost, until some people began to realize that their bread didn't taste like anything.

It all comes down to the industrial revolution and our need to be better, faster and easier. Unfortunately, this value system may have some unintended consequences manifesting in the health of our nation and the rest of the world.

Unfortunately, the bread of today really isn't the bread of our ancient ancestors or even our grandparents.

Is it bread that's making you sick? Or is it what's been done to bread that is making you sick?

- Is it the Vital Wheat Gluten that is now being added to almost every bread on the grocery store shelves?
- Is it the hidden GMOs in the ingredients?
- Is it the breeding methods that have taken place over time that has changed the genetic makeup of wheat that has led to tenfold increases in yields from that of only a century ago?
- Is it the rancidity that takes place in freshly ground whole grain flour that is stored unrefrigerated or the chemical preservatives used to keep it from quickly turning rancid?
- Is it the dough conditioners and additives and artificial colors that are used to help create the illusion of a big bold healthy/hearty/whole grain loaf of bread?
- Is it the synthetic vitamins that are added to replace the ones destroyed in the refinement and milling process?
- Is it the hormone-like substance or "plant growth regulators" that are being applied to the wheat?

- Is it the collection bins sprayed with insecticides and or perhaps it's the fumigation method (a toxic concentration of gas) used to remove any pests from the grain bins?
- Is it poor soil preparation or a lack of a good crop rotation plan?
- Is it the use of herbicides and pesticides?
- Is it the disappearance of the old fashioned stone grinding method that has been replaced by high speed steel roller mills?
- Is it the lack of using a cooled air drying system to dry the grain that causes the protein in the grain to become damaged?
- Is it the preservatives that are added to bread to increase shelf life?

So what is the answer? In reading through all of the above issues one could make a case for any one of them but the answer lies in the whole picture and not just in its individual components. If all of the above weren't bad enough there is one more vital factor to consider.

Lack of Natural Fermentation in Commercial Bread

The original process of natural leavening, slow fermentation, allows the bacteria to break down the carbohydrates and gluten and also neutralizes the phytic acid, making it easier for the body to digest. And, sourdough bread contains healthy resistant starch and doesn't raise blood glucose levels as much as conventional wheat bread.

Beneficial bacteria plays an equally important role in the making of this bread. This puts naturally leavened bread more in the realm of fermented foods such as yogurt and tempeh. Of course, this is nothing new. This is how bread was originally made. If you look at the entire history of bread making, bread made with commercial yeast is really the new thing.

In her book, Nourishing Traditions, Sally Fallon discusses studies by Dr. Weston A. Price. He studied groups of people untouched by civilization. These people have striking health and longevity. This is due, in part, to the fact that they have preserved ancient traditions for food preparation. Dr. Price found that these groups of people – across the board – prepared their grains in one of the following ways: Natural Leavening (sourdough), Sprouting, and Soaking.

There are two methods for leavening bread and they differ totally in the way they act on the flour, as well as on the taste and nutritional effect of the resulting bread and, in the end, on the health of the consumer. The aim of bread fermentation is to transform the various nutrients freed by the milling of the grain and to modify them for optimum assimilation during digestion.

A Definition of Natural Leaven (starter)

Wild yeast, or multi-micro flora are the natural air-borne ferments that are generated or seeded in a dough left exposed to a clean and cool atmosphere under specific conditions of moisture and temperature. Wild yeast also naturally enriches the bread, due to an additional development of nutrients by the beneficial enzymes and ferments.

Fermented bread is bread made from dough that has been allowed to rise slowly using a starter of naturally occurring bacteria and yeast carried in the air. Unlike quick-rising breads that use a single strain of specially cultured, yeast usually sold in packets and called fast-rising or instant yeast, fermented bread contains a variety of yeasts and bacteria that help to convert the important nutrients and sugars in the dough into a form that is more readily digestible than instant yeast breads. The taste, texture and overall character of fermented bread are often markedly different than that of non-fermented breads.

A slow fermentation with natural yeasts and beneficial bacteria from the air creates a different result. The yeast is able to process the ingredients in the bread at a natural rate while also interacting with bacteria and enzymes in the dough, so more nutrients are converted into other forms or are broken down and consumed, i.e. starch and gluten. This results in the gluten in the dough developing into a softer, easy to digest, form than would happen with quick-rising yeast.

There are several health benefits that come from cooking and eating fermented bread. For people who have blood sugar disorders, the glycemic index of fermented bread is considerably less than that of white flour breads made with instant yeast. The digestibility of slow-risen fermented bread also is greater, making it easier on the stomach for people who have slight intolerances to the grains. Natural leavening enables nutrient absorption in the body. The phytic acid is broken down so that our bodies are better able to absorb the nutrients found in grains. Finally, fermented bread is exposed to good bacteria called probiotics that can help promote the health of the digestive system in the body.

Naturally leavening the bread is what turns grain and water into the magical "staff of life"!

Natural leaven bread, because of its inherent beneficial ferments, slowly recreates the population of friendly lactobacillus digestive bacteria in the absorption tract. The end result is a recovery of digestion and proper elimination by the effective action of friendly bacteria.

Gluten (the protein in flour that enables it to stretch as the dough rises) during the fermentation process is partially "digested" making its final digestion by us much easier. When you cut this stage out, people often report a bloated feeling after eating bread.

The glycemic value is lowered by this fermentation process, meaning that the body absorbs the energy over a longer period of time. The bread will have a crisper crust and a chewier crumb and also be likely to stale less quickly.

Additional Benefits:

- Sparking chemical reactions to enrich the natural flavors of whole grains
- Synthesizing vitamins in whole grains to create new nutrients, especially all-important B12
- Boosting amino acid lysine, which is great for vegans because it makes sourdough a nearly complete protein
- Diffusing the phytic acid contained in grains, which helps make minerals like calcium, magnesium, iron and zinc markedly more bioavailable i.e. easy for our intestines to send into our blood streams and on to the organs, hair, skin etc… for great wellness
- Lactic acid, also produced during fermentation, helps promote the growth of healthy flora in the intestines

Consider Homemade Bread

The easiest way to know for sure what's in your bread is to make it yourself. Don't panic! If you can follow directions, you can bake bread.

Talk about bringing love back into the kitchen! Making your own bread is definitely an act of love, but also fun and satisfying. Herbs, sweeteners, spices, raisins, nuts, seeds, and oats may be added for variety. Besides making sourdough bread you can make pizza dough, rolls, pancakes, cakes, biscuits, muffins, crackers and cookies.

If you are not able to bake your own bread find a source which uses very few ingredients, natural leaven (slow ferment), whole grain, water and salt. Bakeries use different terms such as slow rise, long fermentation, sourdough and wild yeast.

But remember it is the slow fermentation process (48 hours is best) that works the magic in breaking down the grain and turning the bread into a healthy food source with great texture.

CHAPTER 19

Slow Fermented Sourdough Bread Recipes

Traditional Sourdough Bread

The fermented dough makes sourdough taste good and is good for your gut. The ancient tradition of fermenting flour and water into sourdough is the magic that makes wheat healthy and "the staff of life" eaten for thousands of years. Many people who have digestive problems, after eating other glutenous foods, don't have the same troubles with long ferment sourdough products. When the millions of fermenting microbes hit your digestive tract it begins to transform your health.

The sourdough process (fermentation) begins with a natural leaven or "starter" consisting of flour and water that are left to ferment. Lactic bacteria and wild yeasts occurring naturally in the environment feed on nutrients in the flour and begin to multiply. These organisms transform or breakdown food components in the flour into a simpler form that is more easily digested and produces carbonic gas causing the dough to rise. This is important for a lighter texture and even, thorough baking.

Your sourdough starter is a method for cultivating wild yeast used for baking that has been used for thousands of years

Sourdough Starter Recipe

Super Loaves & Simple Treats by Melissa Sharp
You will need a glass jar with a screw on lid or a small crock with a loose lid, if it has a plastic sealer, remove it.

Day 1

1 teaspoon white bread flour
1 teaspoon filtered water, room temp or a little warmer, not hot or cold
Mix together with your hands. We all have a little wild yeast on us and this will give your starter a little boost.

Leave the starter out overnight at room temperature. Cover it loosely with the lid. You don't want it to dry out but you want the wild yeasts in the air to get in.

Day 2

Throw away ½ of the starter mixture from day 1
add 1 teaspoon white bread flour
and 1 teaspoon filtered water
Mix together with your hands and leave it out overnight, lightly covered.

Days 3 and 4

Repeat Day 2

Day 5

By now you should see bubbles in your starter. This means it is ready to use. Don't worry if it smells a little cheesy or acidic, this is normal. Each starter will create its own unique aroma. If you don't see bubbles on Day 5, keep repeating Day 2 until you get bubbles. If the temperature in your home is cool it may take longer. Don't give up.

Now you have your own living jar of healthy microbes that you will be using and sharing with your friends for years to come.

How to Use Your Starter

The day before you bake you will need to build up your starter to strengthen it for rising.

Day 1

all of the starter from the jar
6 Tablespoons white bread flour
3 1\2 Tablespoons warm water
Mix together and leave out overnight, loosely covered

Day 2

You will use most of the starter for your recipe. What you don't use, you keep as your ongoing active starter for the next recipe.

- If you use the starter on a regular basis it becomes a part of your bread and baking routine.
- Keep your starter in the refrigerator unless you are using it everyday. Bring it out to refresh it and return it to the refrigerator.
- If you don't use it for a few weeks or a few months it may separate, just stir it back together. To get it going again you want to overwhelm it with food. Throw ½ of the starter away and add 3/4 cup white bread flour and 7 Tablespoons of filtered water. Mix it together and leave it out overnight and it should be active and bubbling again. By throwing

½ of the starter away you are also throwing out ½ of the microorganism so the remaining gets more food. This will make the starter more active more quickly.

- It is quite easy to obtain a sweet tasting bread with a natural leaven fermentation for a base. The slower proofing of the dough at temperatures between 62 and 64 degrees Fahrenheit, made from a leaven always stored at low temperatures of 47 to 50 degrees Fahrenheit and regularly refreshed, will totally prevent the characteristic sour dough taste often associated with natural leavened bread.

Whole Wheat Sourdough Loaf

There are many recipes and methods for making sourdough bread, from simple family-style loaves made with a free standing mixer using a dough hook, to fancy french breads made with the stretch and fold method, molded in baskets and baked in cast iron roasting pans. There are also many grains, combinations of grains, spices, nuts, seeds and sweeteners that can be used for variation.

I bake family style whole wheat sourdough bread loaves for toast and sandwiches once a week and leave the fancy loaves to the bakers. I am a busy woman with modern kitchen appliances that I take full advantage of!

Goddess Sourdough Bread

Whole Wheat Sourdough Bread
Sourdough starter, raw honey, coconut oil, sea salt, and freshly ground wheat create this simple and wholesome loaf.

Ingredients:

- 6-7 cups freshly ground wheat flour (I use hard red winter wheat and hard white wheat at a 50/50 ratio)
- 1 cup fed sourdough starter
- ½ cup melted coconut oil
- 1 tablespoon salt
- ½ cup honey
- 2 cups filtered water

Instructions:

- The night before you want to bake your bread, combine the sourdough starter, oil, salt, honey, and water in a large bowl. (I use a stand mixer with a dough hook for this. You can knead it by hand, but if you plan to make bread loaves regularly, a stand mixer is a great investment for the ease and time it saves.)
- With the mixer running, gradually begin adding flour to the other ingredients, just enough flour until it starts pulling away from the sides of the mixer, or is not sticking to your hands. It will vary between 6 and 7 cups, depending on the hydration of the starter and the type of wheat you use. Add a little more water if it is too dry, or more flour if it is too wet. (When using whole wheat flour the dough needs to be a bit stickier than you think it should be because the flour will continue to absorb the water while it is rising.)
- Knead the dough (about 10 - 15 minutes) until it is stretchy and you can stretch a small piece and thin it out like a transparent window pane, without it breaking. If it breaks apart when stretched it needs more kneading to work the gluten.

- Place the dough in a coconut oil greased glass bowl. Roll the dough around a bit so that the entire ball is lightly coated with coconut oil. This keeps it from drying out and rises better. Cover the dough with a tea towel and let it rise until doubled in size. Time will vary depending on the temperature of the room, may take 4 hours or more. (I mix up my dough before I go to bed and divide it into 2 loaves in the morning. If I get interrupted I put the dough in the fridge until I can get to it.)
- Gently divide the dough into two even balls, stretch the dough over the top to create a little tension, without pressing out all of the air bubbles, and place each one into a coconut oil greased loaf pan, coating the top with a little extra coconut oil, for a softer crust. Lightly cover them with plastic wrap (it likes the humidity) and a tea towel. Place in the refrigerator for 24 to 48 hours to ferment.
- When you are ready to bake, take them out of fridge and set out allowing them to double in size in a warm place, covered with a tea towel. This should take anywhere from 4-12 hours, depending on how warm your kitchen is. If it is cold you can set them in the oven with the light on. (Preheat the oven to 100 degrees then turn off the oven and turn on the light to keep the oven warm.)
- Check to see if they are ready to bake by gently depressing the dough. If it is hard to indent the dough hasn't proofed long enough and needs more rising time. If it quickly springs back and doesn't leave much of an indentation, it is ready to bake. If it leaves an indentation and doesn't spring back it has over-proofed and may be a dense loaf.
- Bake the bread on oven racks for 45 to 60 minutes at 400 degrees. Test for doneness by thumping the bottom of the bread, it should sound hollow. If not, return to oven in the pan or just on the oven rack for a few more minutes. Internal temperature should be 190 to 200 degrees when

the dough is fully cooked. Better to be a little over done than too doughy. Poke the thermometer from the side of the loaf to the middle so you don't mess up the top.

- The baking time will vary depending on how cold the dough is when it goes in the oven. I always use a thermometer to test for doneness because this is a lot of work to end up with doughy bread in the middle. I have put the loaf pans in the oven straight out of the fridge and they rose fine but took almost an hour to bake to 190 degrees, the longer it bakes the darker the crust gets.

Trouble Shooting Sourdough

- Because every person's starter is going to be slightly different, be ready to adapt by adjusting flour or water amounts to suit the consistency of your starter. You want smooth, elastic, not too sticky, but not dry dough.
- Too much salt will hinder the rising of the dough. But no salt leaves the bread lacking, tasting flat.
- The temperature will affect rising time and sour flavor. Cooler temps will give you a mild flavor and warmer temps will be more sour. I like the first ferment setting out on the counter overnight and the second fermenting in the fridge for a day or two. You can experiment and adjust it to your liking.

How Long Will Whole Wheat Sourdough Bread Keep?

Wrap the bread with beeswax wraps, or in a plastic ziplock bag, and store up to two weeks at room temperature.

Fermented whole grain bread keeps longer than unfermented whole grain bread at room temperature.

This is because the fermentation process makes the bread less susceptible to mold and fungus. The same scientific principles that make sauerkraut and lacto fermented salsa keep for several months are at work in the sourdough bread.

The limited growth of friendly lactic bacteria and the presence of other micro-organisms will add little to the acidity, yet will create a good swelling of the gluten as evidenced by small but regular air cells in the crumb. As it ages, natural leavened bread will retain its moisture and keep well without refrigeration, quite opposed from the yeasted bread that stales and dries out within hours after its baking. With natural leaven, no dried out bread need ever to be thrown out.

For longer storage, you can also keep it in the fridge or slice it and put it in the freezer.

Easy No-knead Einkorn Sourdough Bread

This recipe is especially great for people who work full time, it takes 10 minutes in the morning to throw this together and then it's ready to bake 8-12 hours later. You could also throw this together at night, and bake in the morning.

Makes one 3-1/2 lb loaf of bread

Ingredients:

- 1 cup or more* proofed/bubbling sourdough starter
- 6 cups Einkorn flour
- 2 to 3 cups room temp filtered water
- 1 tbsp sea salt
- 1/2 tsp citric acid, totally optional, it's to increase the sour flavor. You can also add some flavoring ingredients such as rosemary, asiago… whatever. Get creative!

- 1 cup of starter is all that's needed, but if you add more, you'll get a more sour-tasting bread. Just use a little less water if you're using extra starter.

Instructions:

1. In a large bowl (preferably one that has a lid), add the flour, sourdough starter, water and salt and mix until blended. It should be a gluey thick batter, a little thicker than brownie batter.

2. Cover and let it rise in a warm spot for about 8+ hours, or until bubbly and doubled in size. In the winter, I turn my oven light on for warmth and keep the bowl in the oven for rising.

3. Once the dough has risen sufficiently (8-12 hours, depending on ambient temps), remove it from the oven. Place your empty covered casserole in the oven and set the oven temp 450 degrees F.

4. Once temp is achieved, remove your casserole from the oven. CAUTION: HOT HOT HOT! Remove the lid and gently pour the dough into the casserole, being careful to not disturb too many bubbles. Cover and bake for 60 minutes. PLEASE NOTE: You may have to experiment with bake time due to altitude differences. Being at almost 6,000 ft., you may need to bake for 80 minutes.

5. Remove the bread from the oven and remove lid. After 10-15 minutes, dump the bread out of the casserole, place on a cooling rack and allow it to cool completely before slicing and serving. I usually leave it on the counter over night to cool and dry a little and then cut it in the morning with a meat slicer.

Stone Age Bread

There are heaps of versions of this Nordic / Viking / Stone Age bread. This Nut & Seed Bread is the bomb! Gluten free, paleo, keto, packed with filling nuts and seeds, it's portable, sturdy enough to carry a huge serving of smashed avocado.

This isn't technically a "bread" but it can be used like a bread. No flour, yeast or sourdough needed.

Ingredients:

- 3.5 oz pumpkin seeds
- 3.5 oz sunflower seeds
- 3.5 oz almonds
- 3.5 oz walnuts
- 3.5 oz linseed/flax seeds
- 3.5 oz sesame seeds
- 5 eggs
- 1/2 cup olive oil or coconut oil
- 2 tsp salt

Instructions:

- Soak the nuts in filtered water for at least 4 hours. Drain and Rinse.
- In a large bowl; Mix the soaked nuts, seeds and salt. Use the nuts, grains and seeds as they are OR you can chop them.
- In a small bowl mix together the eggs and oil. Pour mixture over the nuts and seeds and mix well to thoroughly incorporate the eggs and oil into all of the nut and seeds.
- Cut out a sheet of parchment paper so that it just covers the bottom of a normal bread pan. Pour the dough into the pan. Press down, shape the loaf and smooth the top with a spatula.

- Do not preheat the oven. Place the bread pan on the bottom rack. You want the mixture to start to bake slowly as the heat rises so that it cooks through.
- Bake the bread at 350 degrees for one hour. You'll know it's done when the top is lightly golden, and when you press down on the middle of the loaf and it feels solid and compact. If it's still springy to the touch, bake it a bit longer.
- Let the bread cool completely before removing from the pan. Let cool on a cooling rack before eating.
- Slice thinly with a very sharp knife and serrate back and forth to cut through the solid nuts. Don't push down or you'll get nowhere and risk crumbling everything.
- Delicious toasted or not, topped with smoked salmon, or crumbled feta, smashed avocado, or peanut butter, or even some plain butter and a pinch of salt.
- Store in an airtight container for a week. Freeze any left over slices and thaw by toasting

Notes:

You can pretty much mix it together and have it in the oven in 10 minutes or less. It is also really versatile so you can experiment with a variety of seeds and nuts, and also switch out the olive oil for coconut oil.

In researching this bread I found out that the magic number for the ingredients is 600g, so you can create so many different varieties of the bread by mixing and matching the nuts, seeds, and even dried fruit (each choice needs to weigh 50g until you get to 600g). As long as you keep the same amount of linseeds (flax seed), eggs and oil, the recipe will bind together.

Variations

Try out some of these flavor combinations to change the taste of the bread to your liking. You really can use any combination of nuts and seeds you have. Sometimes I purposefully go shopping for nuts to make this, other times I scavenge the fridge for whatever nuts we have and needs eating to throw in.

Sweet:

- Cinnamon Sugar: 1 teaspoon of cinnamon, 1 tablespoon coconut sugar
- Vanilla: ½ teaspoon vanilla powder, 1 tablespoon coconut sugar
- Cinnamon Spice: 1 teaspoon cinnamon, ¼ teaspoon nutmeg, ¼ teaspoon ground ginger
- Fruity: ¼ cup dried fruit e.g. sultanas, currents, raisins, blueberries, finely chopped fig
- Choc Orange: 50g raw cacao nibs, ½ teaspoon vanilla powder, zest of 1 orange

Savory:

- Sun-dried Tomato & Rosemary: 50g finely diced sun-dried tomatoes, 1 teaspoon dried rosemary
- Fennel: 1 teaspoon whole fennel seeds
- Turmeric and Coriander: 1 teaspoon turmeric powder, ½ teaspoon ground coriander
- Garlic and Thyme: 1 teaspoon garlic powder, 1 teaspoon dried thyme
- Lemon, Pepper and Garlic: Zest of 1 whole lemon, 2 garlic cloves crushed, ½ teaspoon black pepper
- Italian Olive: 50g finely chopped Kalamata olives, 1 teaspoon Italian seasoning

Fermented Raw Vegan Bread

Chef Ito and Russell James recipe

A soft and spongy raw vegan fermented flax bread that's made into a loaf and can be cut into slices, with a crust! It also has the benefit of being made with fermented flax.

To be raw, food is not heated over 115 degrees to keep the nutrition in tact and not kill the natural enzymes and good bacteria. This bread is made in a food dehydrator.

Ingredients:

Fermented Flax

- 1/4 cup golden flax (ground)
- 2 tsp white miso
- ½ tsp sea salt
- 1 cup water

Bread

- 3/4 cup buckwheat (soaked 1 hour and optionally sprouted 10-12 hours)
- 1/3 cup almond butter
- 2 zucchini (courgette)
- 1 tbsp onion powder
- 1 tsp garlic powder
- 3 tbsp nutritional yeast
- 1 tsp apple cider vinegar
- 1/4 cup honey (or maple)
- 1/4 cup olive oil (or any cold pressed nut oil)
- 1/4 cup fermented flax (from part 1 of the recipe)
- 1/4 cup psyllium husk
- 3/4 cup almonds ground

- 2 tbsp coconut flour

Instructions:

Fermented Flax

- Blend all ingredients together.
- Close the jar and ferment at a warm room temperature for 10-15 hours.
- Once ready store in the fridge and use within 4 days.

Bread

- In a high speed blender combine the first set of ingredients (leave out the last 4 ingredients in the list for now) and blend on high until smooth.
- Add the psyllium and fermented flax and pulse in the blender just to incorporate. (It is the psyllium that makes this raw bread recipe spongy and good. YOU MUST USE PSYLLIUM or this recipe won't work.
- In a bowl, mix together the last 2 ingredients with your hands.
- Add the contents of the blender to the mixing bowl with the flours and mix well with your hands to combine.
- Allow the mix to sit 2 minutes, during this time it will firm up as the psyllium and coconut flour absorb moisture.
- Form the dough into a log and dehydrate on a nonstick sheet for 8-10 hours at 115F. Remove from nonstick and dry again for 8-10 hours. Slice the bread and dehydrate again to dry the inside, about 2 hours.
- Alternatively, line a baking tin with a strip of greaseproof paper and press the dough in. Use a little water to smooth the edges and get the look that you want.

- Dry at 115F for 8-10 hours. Remove from the tin by pulling up on the strips of greaseproof paper. If it's stuck, be sure there are no dry bits on top sticking to the mold.
- Dry again for 8-10 hours before slicing and drying one last time for an hour or so to get the inside dry to the amount you like.

SECTION THREE

Survival Skills

CHAPTER 20

Lost Survival Skills

When you think about it, the matter of survival is not that different today from 500 years ago, or even 5,000 years ago.

Our bodies look and behave like the bodies of our ancestors millennia ago. Our brains have also essentially remained unaltered for millennia. And the six things that killed humans 5,000 years ago are the same six things that kill people today.

- Getting too hot
- Getting too cold
- Thirst
- Hunger
- Illness
- Injury

To survive, our ancestors developed skills to protect them from these threats. This skill development took place over hundreds of generations of trial and error. Many of these "survival skills", or life skills, were common knowledge up until just a few generations ago. In the past century so much knowledge has been lost. But much has been gained too, of course. Today, we require an entirely new set of skills to get by, but at the expense of our ancient know-how.

These skills that kept our foremothers and forefathers alive are forgotten today in the sense that they're no longer general knowledge. They've been forgotten because modern humans require another set of skills to survive, like how to make a steady income, drive a car, and stay on the right side of the law.

Modern lifestyle has turned people into highly-dependent beings; whether it's dependency towards the car, towards the supermarkets, towards politicians, towards centralized infrastructure. Our modern infrastructure shields us from threats to our lives, and as long as everything works it's all fine and dandy. But, as countless examples from history and more recent times show, when you're dependent on things outside of your control and these things stop working, the people affected by the disruption or disaster are in for a rude awakening.

As a culture we have put all of our eggs in one basket and learned to depend on industry and technology to provide for our needs. This system is very fragile, far more fragile than any of us realize right now. One major disaster that interrupted our power supply, communication, or transportation, could send us back to a time where we would have to depend on these very same skills. We do not have to wonder IF it will happen, as much as asking when it will happen.

Are You Prepared For An Emergency?

The experts in disaster preparedness and response, FEMA and Red Cross, both state that families should keep a minimum of 72-hours of survival supplies in their home. These agencies are even going so far as to recommend people increase their food and water supplies to last 10 – 14 days. Most of us could survive for a few weeks with the surplus food and supplies we already have at home, but if there was major disaster how long could you survive and take care of yourself?

- Are you prepared for an emergency?
- If we were in an emergency situation that lasted months or a few years could you survive?
- Do you have a plan if you loose electricity for an extended time?
- If the trucks weren't bringing food to the grocery store, how long could you and your family survive?
- Do you have money put away for an emergency if you couldn't get any money out of the bank?
- If you lost clean running water, do you know how to purify water for drinking?

Water

A reliable and regular supply of water is a true necessity of life. In the developed world you likely get your water from a tap; a relatively new invention and far from resilient.

Finding Drinking Water

- What are the best places to find drinkable water?
- How do I know if it's drinkable?
- What can I do to minimize the risk of drinking foul water?

Purifying Water

- In what ways can I purify water?
- How do I make active charcoal for water purification?

Well Building

- How do I build a durable well?
- How do I know where to start digging?

Moving Water With Gravity

- How do I move water from place A to place B using only gravity?
- How do I move water uphill without using electricity?

First Aid

- How do I clean and disinfect a wound?
- How do I dress a wound?
- How do I stop heavy bleeding?
- How do I perform CPR?
- How do I splint a broken leg / hand / finger / toe / back / neck?
- How do I close an open wound using suturing?

Making Soap

- What materials do I need to make soap?

Herbal Medicine

- Which plants can I use to treat X?
- How do I turn those plants into usable extracts, oils, balms, teas and tinctures?

Candle Making

- How do I make candles from tallow?
- How do I make candles from bees wax?
- How do I make stearin?
- Which materials make good wicks?

Food

A reliable and regular supply of food is a true necessity of life. Chances are you get your food from a supermarket. Well, here's a sobering fact: If food trucks stopped delivering to your supermarket, for example due to a natural disaster or financial meltdown, the store shelves will be empty within 48 hours. So it might just be worth it to learn some of the skills below.

Foraging / Knowing What To Eat

- What wild plants, berries, fruits, roots, nuts and mushrooms grow in my area that I can eat without getting killed?
- Which of them are in season now?

Cooking From Scratch

- How do I cook without electricity?
- How do I cook using a dutch oven?
- How do I cook over an open fire?
- How do I make something taste good without following a recipe?
- What spices should I use when?

Baking Bread

- How do I make flour?
- How do I "make" yeast?
- How do I bake bread without electricity?

Preserving Food

- How do I can food?
- How do I dehydrate food?
- How do I ferment food?

- How do I smoke food?
- How do I salt food?

Gardening

- What kind of plants / vegetables / root crops / berries / fruits can I grow in my area?
- How do I know when to plant things?
- How do I make compost?
- How do I minimize weeds?
- Can I eat the weeds?
- How do I make biochar?
- How do I get started?

Orchard Management

- How do I plant a tree to give it the best possible start in life?
- How do I prune a tree?
- How do I propagate trees through seeds?
- How do I propagate trees through grafting?
- How do I manage diseases and pests?

Seed Saving

- How do I save seeds from X plant?
- How do I store seeds?
- How do I stratify seeds to get them to germinate better?

Home Brewing

- How do I make beer / wine / mead?
- From where can I get the yeast?
- How do I save the yeast until next time?
- How do I control the alcohol percentage?

Once you learn a new skill, practice it, then learn another skill! I think we can learn a lot from our foremothers, not just about surviving to live another day but also about thriving and finding meaning in this day and age.

Emergency Preparedness Skills

- Plan for alternative ways to cook without public power such as a wood cookstove, solar oven, or open fire, in case the grid goes down.
- Master fire starting in all types of conditions so that you can cook and keep yourself and family warm in a grid down situation.
- Store water and implement a plan for continuous water.
- Stockpile staple foods and supplies which you can't produce easily on your property.
- Learn to bake bread and make a sourdough starter.
- Purchase dried beans instead of canned beans.
- Eliminate addictive or bad habits so that you won't be dependent on something like cigarettes or alcohol which will be scarce and pricey in times of turmoil.

Self-Reliance Skills for Daily Life

- Create an emergency fund of accumulated cash to cover your expenses for 3 to 6 months or longer so you can survive any kind of short term personal economic hardship.
- Reduce monthly expenses by cutting out the services that you don't absolutely need. Prioritize needs over wants and put extra money into savings or use to pay down debt.
- Pay down debt as much as possible with a goal of becoming debt free.
- Wait a week before you make a large purchase unless it's an emergency.

- Begin composting to lower the amount of waste that you must dispose of and to enhance soil for gardening.
- Stop using disposable items such as paper towels, paper plates, etc. Although they are more convenient, they cost more money. Invest in linen napkins, hand towels, and washable plates and use these instead.
- Learn to DIY things you need so you can save money now and be able to make what you need in a grid down or economic collapse scenario.
- Hang insulating curtains in your windows to save energy.
- Install awnings, trellis, or an arbor to keep the home cooler in summer.
- Add extra insulation in your attic to reduce energy costs.
- Reduce the size of your lawn to save on water and gas for the lawnmower and lawn care services.

Learn to be happy with less. Sometimes, when we slow down and learn to appreciate the little things, we realize that maybe these are actually the big things in life.

CHAPTER 21

Urban Homesteading in an Apartment, Condo or Rental

So, you stay in the city and you like your urban lifestyle. Yet you also like the idea of being self-sufficient, growing your own food, and eating organic and local, like you live on a farm.

What is homesteading? It is nothing but a lifestyle of self sufficiency. It involves many things such food preservation, agriculture, raising animals for food, maintaining your own house and property yourself, sewing and making household items, and generally living off the land.

When you live in a rental, condo, or apartment, this may be a tall order. You probably don't have any "land" or there are strict rules governing what you can do on your property. In general your space is limited. Despite these limitations there are numerous ways in which you can embrace urban homesteading right now in your apartment. Here's how:

Cook Your Own Food

Forget the processed stuff that comes in a box or can and forget the takeout place down the road. Cook healthy local foods from scratch. Fresh local food will nourish your body and minimize the chance you will have medical bills. It is also a great step towards self sufficiency.

Buy From The Farm

You probably don't have room to raise a grass fed cow or pasture a pig. You may not have room to grow pumpkin vines. You can source local organic farms in your area though and support them. They need the support and you want the farm fresh goodies. It's a win, win. Find a place where you can get farm fresh pastured eggs weekly. You can eat like you live off the land even if you don't.

Have A Porch Garden

If you're in an apartment or rental chances are you do have a little space to grow. You can have a nice little garden with pots and herbs and grow peppers, tomatoes, onions, lettuce, garlic and strawberries. You can also have your very own compost bin on the porch so that you will be able to get fresh compost when you need it and at the same time reduce the amount of garbage you create.

You can sprout seeds on your kitchen counter, grow microgreens and wheat grass on shelves for fresh and inexpensive greens year round.

I think I can say with a degree of certainty that you'll never be able to grow enough food in your apartment for you to live off of without turning your entire home into a jungle. However, that doesn't mean that you can't grow some of your own food while still keeping your home a home, rather than an expensive greenhouse.

Try "Alternative" Gardening

- Maybe you don't have much of a porch and you don't have a balcony.
- Search your area for a community garden or a backyard sharing program. The former will rent you a small plot of land to use for your garden and the latter is an opportunity to help someone cultivate their space and you share in the bounty.
- There is also wild food foraging. You can find edibles like fruit trees on abandoned properties or public spaces (like parks) and scoop up the harvest when it is ready.
- One step further is guerrilla gardening. You find land that is not being cared for…empty lots, foreclosed homes, areas of public properties that are not well traveled, etc and you grow food stealthily. During early spring do some quick planting or throw some seed bombs and then return in a bit to see what happens. You may have a new food source!

Embrace Natural Remedies

Learn some of the well known natural cures for common ailments and keep and herbal medicine box at hand so that you are able to treat yourself and your family for those little aches and pains that inevitably occur. You can treat colds, flu, fevers, tummy aches, poison ivy, cuts, eczema, head lice, etc. all from the comfort of your home.

Make Your Own Personal Care Products

When you live in a homesteading environment, you will be able to minimize your shopping bill as you go about making your own natural body and skin care products. This kind of hobby is fun and the resulting products are much safer than the toxic ones you buy in stores. So stop wasting money on chemical laden junk and make your own toothpaste, deodorant, moisturizer, and even makeup. The possibilities are endless.

Make Your Own Cleaning Products

It is simple and you need only a few basic affordable ingredients. Then you can stop wasting money on expensive store bought products. Purchase some baking soda, vinegar, Castile soap, lemons, coconut oil, and a few essential oils and you have the makings of just about any cleaning product. Castile soap alone has a ton of household uses.

Can, Preserve, Ferment And Dehydrate Food

When you live in a homesteading environment you typically store seasonal foods for use later in the year when they are not available. Canning, dehydrating, fermenting, and otherwise preserving foods when they are local and in season is something you can do just about anywhere as long as you have the space.

If you are new to this concept then start with canning. Get some supplies and can one or two crops to start. Increase what you do each year until you have steady supply of foods to tide you over when the weather is cold.

These are some simple homesteading practices that will help you learn the art of self sufficiency, even if you live in the city and you have no land to speak of.

CHAPTER 22

Preparing for an Emergency

"Self-reliance is the only road to true freedom,
and being one's own person is its
ultimate reward" Patricia Sampson

I'm not a "survivalist" but I'm not an idiot either. We must prepare for natural and man-made disasters because they are inevitable and yet completely beyond our control. Disasters pose a significant threat to our lives, our homes, our communities, our environment, and the economy. The effects they have can be devastating and long-lasting.

While we cannot prevent disasters from happening, we can reduce their risk by becoming prepared. Our response to these events is critical for lessening their impact and overcoming residual challenges, as well as accelerating the process of recovery.

Emergency situations are stressful. When we're put under a lot of stress, our brains don't think clearly. Having a family preparedness plan is necessary because it allows you to determine the best course of action to take before an event occurs. That way when something does happen, your mind is focused and ready to confront it.

As a culture we tend to live in the moment. While in one sense this is not a bad thing, but when living in the moment means not thinking about potential outcomes in our future, we are at risk of leaving ourselves and our children ill-prepared to meet their future.

History shows that disasters do happen, and when they do, will future generations have the skills they need to weather those disasters? I have heard so many people say, "that will never happen". Perhaps not in our lifetime, but eventually? The odds are against us.

Do you want to be better prepared for emergencies but aren't sure where to start or if you're doing it right? Whether you're worried about a sudden layoff, home invasions, car accidents, the power going out for a week, natural disasters, or long term economic and societal decline, it's critical that you start getting prepared now. By definition, if you wait until you need it, it's already too late. It's easy to prepare for a food shortage in calmer times because everything is available.

The whole point of preparing is to reduce the chances of major life disruptions and to better recover from disruptions when they do happen. That's it. Even something as simple and common as a fire extinguisher in your kitchen counts. The vast majority of "prepping" has nothing to do with bunkers and bullets.

The basic steps to prepping:

- Build a solid personal finance and health foundation
- Get your home ready for two weeks of self-reliance
- Be able to leave your home with only a moment's notice ("bug out bags")
- Prepare for emergencies that happen away from home ("get home bags")

Your goal is to be able to survive in your home for at least two weeks without any outside help. That means you can't assume you'll have electricity, water, cooking or heating gas, communication, internet, 911, ambulances, and so on.

Modern experts believe you should be prepared for at least two weeks in order to handle the majority of likely events. Some groups, like the Red Cross, have updated their suggestions; their site now says, "3-day supply for evacuation, 2-week supply for home."

It's wrong to think "my plan is to bug out" or "my plan is to shelter in place at home". Emergencies don't care about your plans, and a good prep means being able to do both.

Why Being Self-Sufficient Matters

Our grandparents and great-grandparents knew the importance of being self-sufficient. They survived an economic depression and major wars so they fostered age-old skills, just in case.

These days, we are a few generations removed from crisis, and we are heavily dependent on products that make our lives easier. This lack of perspective coupled with reliance on convenience means we're one thing and one thing only: Vulnerable.

Our well-being is dramatically affected by things we can't control: weather, inflation, politics, etc. Preparing for job loss or sudden illness isn't futile; it's smart. And when it comes to climate change? As devastating storms increase in frequency we may find ourselves relying on our great-grandparents' long-lost skills to get us through.

How much food would you need to feed yourself and family for 3 days, 3 weeks or 3 months if food wasn't available at the grocery stores or you couldn't get to the store?

How much water would you need for drinking, cooking, washing, etc. if there was no running water to your home for 3 days, 3 weeks or three months?

How many products like toilet paper, paper towels, paper plates, and garbage bags might you need?

How much laundry soap, toothpaste, feminine hygiene products, medication, and first aid supplies would you need if the store shelves were empty?

What would you need for cooking, warmth, and electrical dependent equipment if there was no electricity to your home for 3 days, 3 weeks or 3 months?

I'm not trying to be a scare monger or suggest you need to become a "prepper" or live off the grid but I am suggesting you consider storing extra food, candles, matches, flashlights, batteries, solar powered back-up, etc just in case you find yourself in an emergency situation, be it a natural disaster, you become injured or ill, loose your job, or any other unforseen catastrophe.

It is much better to be prepared for an emergency and never have one. It is like insurance, hopefully you never need to use it but if you do, thank goodness you have it! May we learn from our ancient Divine Feminine ancestors; to prepare for the worst of times, hope for the best of times and live in peace each day knowing we are prepared, rather than living in fear .

If you are new to the idea of food storage and preparing for a disaster, the following can be over whelming. In terms of priority, you will want to focus on these items:

- Water
- Food
- Medicine/Prescriptions
- Toilet paper + buckets for toilet
- Lighting
- Heating/Warmth
- First Aid
- Hygiene items

As you can see self-reliance is a journey, and it doesn't happen overnight, but it requires a new mindset.

Extra Food Storage

With food being so convenient and easy to buy we don't usually think about stocking up too much at one time. But the political upheaval, climate change, storms, earthquakes, fires, unemployment and the covid-19 health pandemic has reminded us of the importance of being prepared in case of an unexpected emergency. There are many possible emergency situations we could find ourselves in and it is our Divine Feminine responsibility to prepare for the safety of ourselves and our families. It would not be very Divine to find yourself unprepared, helpless and at the mercy of others if you could have prepared but didn't.

Even if you are planning to raise a lot of your own food, it's wise to have a stockpile of food in case a drought or other situation limits your food production.

Calculating Your Food Storage:

Trying to guess how much food you'll need for meals next week is a pretty daunting task, so can you imagine what it is like to calculate how much food you need for a month, 3 months or a year?

Track Your Meals:

This method allows you to track what you eat already, then breaking it down by ingredients and tracking over the number of months you want to stock up for. It will be specific to your family's needs, dietary requirements or simply food preference issues.

Here's the idea: We'll take this a step at a time to make it easy, and you'll find that it comes quickly once you get the ball rolling.

- Take your family's favorite meal.
- Write out the recipe X 3 (that's 3 months worth of that meal if you have it once a month).

- Buy enough of that product to stock your pantry for 3 months for that meal.
- Do it again for the next meal.

First In First Out Model: "Store what you use, use what you store". It's an easy way to build up your home supplies without extra cost or effort, and applies to water, food, and daily consumables like toilet paper and batteries.

Food isn't as critical as water since most people can survive weeks without it. So, for your basic short-term emergency coverage, the first line of defense is to just have some extra shelf-stable food on hand.

Each time you go to the store get a little extra to begin building up your supply. Only store foods you normally eat. Neither you or your family will eat food you don't like or aren't use to eating it so don't waste your money on commercially prepared food storage that takes up room and will never get eaten.

Rotate your food like they do in the markets with the newest purchased groceries in the back, moving them forward as you buy more. Write expiration dates on products, to include frozen items, as needed so nothing gets forgotten and goes to waste.

Organize your pantry: This is a good time to organize your storage spaces with space saving items like bins, baskets, tiered shelving, lazy susans, labels, etc.

Here's a secret: When you have accumulated a decent amount of stored food (a deep pantry, full chest freezer, dry goods, etc., basically your own mini grocery store), then you will have the luxury of (mostly) buying only when something's on sale.

If you mostly eat foods from your stored food inventory, you won't be forced to grocery shop for "needs". Your needs will already be in your home. Thus, you can be picky about your shopping and buying items when they are on sale and in season, etc.

Store extra seeds for your garden and don't forget about your pets needs. It's also wise to have some cash on hand in case you can't get it out of the bank when needed.

Water Storage

"Once you carry your own water you will learn the value of every drop"

Water is just too important to leave to chance. So don't assume you'll have time to fill the bathtub or run to the store, and don't use inappropriate vessels such as milk jugs. Get proper water storage tanks/containers instead.

Calculating your water storage: The bare minimum recommendation is 1 gal. of water per person per day, but you'll need to plan to store more and make plans on how to acquire more in the event of an emergency. Store 15 gallons of potable water per person (roughly 1 gallon per day) and have ways to treat dirty water via either bleach, a portable water filter or countertop water filter.

If commerce were disrupted by either a natural or man made disaster, one of the first things a person should do is evaluate their water situation. This involves three different but related issues:

1. How much water is on hand right now?
2. Where can more water be obtained?
3. How can that water be made safe to drink?

The three basic necessities which sustain life are:

1. air
2. water
3. food

The Rule of Threes states that a person can live for:

three-minutes without air, three-days without water, and three-weeks without food.

Without water or any other fluids, a person will die in about three days. Therefore, since water is one of life's most basic necessities, it is a subject we should not take for granted.

Some Interesting Facts About Water and The Human Body

The Human Body:

- 60% of our body is water.
- 75% of our brain is water.
- 83% of our blood is water and it transports nutrients and oxygen to the cells of our body.
- Our urine is almost all water and it is how our body flushes and rids itself of toxic wastes.
- Water facilitates normal bowel movements which helps prevent constipation.
- In one day the average person loses between 2 to 3 quarts of water through their urine, sweat, and normal breathing. If a person doesn't replace that lost water, then dehydration begins to occur.
- At 2% dehydration, thirst is perceived.
- At 5% dehydration, a person becomes hot and tired, and strength and endurance decrease.
- At 10% dehydration, delirium and blurred vision become a problem.
- At 20% dehydration, a person dies.

Pause and reflect on that for a moment. A person loses 2 to 3 quarts of water every day as a result of their normal body functions. Which means if a person doesn't get any fluids for about three days, they will die.

Most people have never thought about the above because they

have never been personally confronted with a extended shortage of fresh safe drinking water at any time in their lives.

Some More Facts About Water:

- Water is VERY heavy.
- One gallon of water weighs about 8.5 pounds inside a thin-walled clear plastic water jug.
- You can't carry enough water with you between locations to last for very long.

Hot Water Heaters: Most hot water heaters contain 40 gallons of clean water. However, BEFORE you remove that water you MUST turn off the power or turn off the gas to your hot water heater, or you could start a fire. Then open the faucet at the bottom of the water heater to gain immediate access to 40 gallons of reserve clean drinking water. This is enough emergency water to last a family of four for 20 days if they ONLY drink the water and don't wash with it. This is the best source of reserve drinking water for the average family because it is constantly being used and replaced inside the hot water heater prior to the emergency. Therefore it will be fresh and clean at the beginning of an emergency. (Note: Some hot water heaters do NOT have an easy access water value at their base. Prior to an emergency you should take a look at your hot water heater and determine if you can get to the water inside your heater. If you can't, then you might consider having a plumber install a standard water faucet value in the water line at the bottom of the hot water heater.)

Bath Tub: If you have warning of an impending disaster you may have time to fill up th bath tub with clean water.

If you had the foresight to plan for an unexpected emergency, then you should have a stash of clean empty 2-liter plastic soda bottles stored somewhere out-of-sight. They are really nice for storing water because they are free, they are made of food grade plastic, they don't leak, they have a screw on cap to keep the water clean, they have an extremely long shelf life, and they are a convenient size to handle and use. The major disadvantage of the 2-liter bottles is that don't stack well on top of one another.

If you have empty one-gallon plastic water jugs then you should also consider saving them for a future emergency. However, clean empty plastic milk jugs are NOT a good option because they will deteriorate with the passage of time and begin to leak.

Another source of water is canned foods because many canned foods are packed in water. When you open a can, serve the water in the can with the food. Never throw the canned water away if you are low on water.

Water that isn't safe to drink is toilet tank water and water inside the mattress of a water bed.

Ration Water

After inventorying your water, the next step is to ration your water. During normal times, one person consumes about 3 quarts of water per day. All of us drink some water, plus a variety of other fluids (coffee, tea, soda, juice, or whatever appeals to you). During hardship conditions, a person can survive on two quarts of water per day (two quarts is one-half gallon). If water is really in short supply, then one quart per day will keep a person alive, but they will begin to slowly dehydrate.

Everyone knows better, but after an extended period of time with little or no water, a person will drink all the water they can when it suddenly becomes available. If you do this, you will get sick. Force yourself to slow down. Drink one cup of water every 10 minutes. Give your system a chance to absorb the water and send it where it is needed most. Don't overload your system and make yourself ill.

Non-Food Storage Items

There are non-food items you need to have in your home storage if you want to really be prepared for an emergency. Stockpiling food isn't going to be enough to get you through a long-term disaster.

Here is a list of non-food items you will need to stockpile.

1. Toilet Paper: Look for it on sale and stock up. We have supplies of it under every bathroom counter and in storage, under the stairs and in other places you might not even think to look for toilet paper. We learned from the Covid pandemic you don't want to get caught without extra toilet paper in your storage.

2. Pain relievers, medicines, prescriptions: There's nothing worse than being sick and not having the first aid supplies you need.

3. Batteries: Take a look at the most common battery needs for your household and get some of every size, AAA to D. Conserve batteries with LED flashlights and lanterns which have a huge advantage over incandescent models: They allow batteries to last much longer (typically about six to 10 times as long).

4. Turn your car into a generator: A power inverter, which turns DC current from your car into AC current for electric gadgets, is the next best thing to a generator when it comes to surviving a blackout. Small units can recharge your computer or phone. Larger ones can power a fridge or power tools.

5. Duct tape, rope, WD40: There are so many uses for these, it's amazing. From tent hole repairs, to bandages, to cloths lines.

6. Paper goods: Having a supply of paper plates, cups, towels and plastic utensils can be invaluable when the power is

out. Keeping paper goods handy means I don't have to worry about washing dishes during a power outage. It also comes in handy when unexpected guests drop by.

7. Plastic zip bags: Heavy duty, freezer strength storage bags are best and can sometimes be reused. You can freeze meals flat and then stand them up on end, they are a top space saver item in the freezer. Zip bags are also great to use in your emergency kits. I can't think of a better way to keep things separated and protected from water and mishaps.

8. Soap: Keep some good old bar soap on hand. Along with frequent hand washing, it is your most effective weapon in fighting germs. Better yet, get supplies to make your own soap and learn how to do it.

Forget the pricey cleaning supplies. You can clean just about anything as long as you have white vinegar and baking soda. Stock up on the big 5# bags of baking soda and gallons of white vinegar from stores like Costco. There are recipes online for homemade laundry detergent using Borax, washing soda and fels naptha soap. It is not difficult to make bar soap, liquid soap and laundry soap.

9. Contractor trash bags: There are about as many uses for a trash bag as there are for duct tape. I'm talking about the black, heavy duty, contractor ones that you can purchase at home repair stores. You can make rope from it, build a tent to stay dry or clean-up a mess in an emergency.

10. Tarps: Another multi-functional preparedness item, the tarp is invaluable for protecting you, and your things, from the elements. You can even make a sail.

11. Feminine products: Unless you want to go back to the way it was done in the olden days, you should store some additional pads and tampons. The pads we use today were

developed as bandages, to absorb the blood of war wounds and can still be used for this purpose.

12. Water purification: Bleach (Use 16 drops of regular household liquid bleach per gallon of water. Do not use scented or color safe bleaches, or those with added cleaners), portable counter top filters, straw filters.

13. Odds and Ends:

- Pairs of scissors, large and small
- Can opener and bottle opener
- Sharpie marker
- Water/fire safe box for important documents
- Emergency cell phone
- Toothbrushes and toothpaste
- Shaving cream and razors
- Face masks
- Hand sanitizer
- Heavy duty aluminum foil
- Whistle

How Reliant We Are On The Grid

The grid is a very old and fragile system, and to be this reliant on something so fickle is a big problem. As we move further along in the climate change timeline, I feel it's necessary to build in some resilience with these systems. With climate change happening, we're going to have more wild weather.

We could manage a power outage of a few days, maybe even a week. But much beyond that would be difficult, or close to impossible for most people.

It's easy enough to stock up on some non-perishable, or easy to heat up foods. But what happens when that stuff runs out? What happens when we've emptied out all the water jugs we filled up?

Common Causes of Power Outages

A power outage can occur anytime there is an interruption in the energy company's system or equipment. This happens most frequently during weather-related incidents such as lightning, ice, wind, tornadoes, hurricanes, and rain or flooding. Vehicle or construction accidents and animal mischief can also cause power outages. Electrical blackouts can also happen, however, these events are not very common as they are mostly due to a major energy company electrical equipment failure.

In case of a power outage, make sure you have many shelf stable foods. We have a Barbeque and heavy duty aluminum foil to cook on the BBQ or in the fire pit, but in case it's cold outside, having something to use indoors like a camp stove, to cook with pots and pans is a life saver. A butane stove is great to have for camping and also insures you can still cook indoors. They are actually very affordable.

Fridge and Freezer:

As far as the food in your fridge and freezer, avoid opening your fridge as much as possible as this will extend the life of your food. Keep ice packs frozen so that you can move some of your stuff into a cooler if you need to.

One of the worst parts of bad storms that take out your electricity for a few hours or days isn't the repairs or damage, it's dealing with your refrigerator and freezer when you haven't had power to keep it cool.

With a few simple steps you can prepare your fridge and freezer for power outages and hopefully save the food inside.

1. **Reorganize your fridge and freezer**

In order to keep your food frozen or cool you need to move the items closer to each other. A tightly packed fridge or freezer can save food for up to two days but a bare fridge will only keep food safely cool for about half a day.

Move all items off of the doors and onto the shelves, tightly packed together. If you have large open spaces and expect your power to be out for more than a few hours pack those areas with newspaper.

If you have two freezers, put your high priority items in one freezer and your easier/cheaper to replace items in the other freezer. The high priority freezer should be packed as tightly as possible and never opened until power is restored.

Move any food that can be frozen, such as milk and meat, from the refrigerator to the freezer to keep it at a safe temperature for longer.

While you're reorganizing your freezer and fridge chances are that you'll find old food that you want to discard. Do not discard it since that would create open space. Use a permanent marker to make X's on the packaging to remind yourself to throw it out once the storm has passed.

2. **Use bottles and containers to freeze ice**

Your refrigerator and freezer will act like a giant ice chest when the power is out. The key is that you simply have to add ice.

Dig through your recycle bin and gather old water bottles or milk jugs to fill with water. Draw giant X's on the bottles to keep people from drinking the water and freeze them. As the storm approaches, move some of the frozen water bottles to the refrigerator and push the other frozen bottles into any open spots in the freezer.

The more ice you add, the longer your food items will remain cool and safe.

3. Don't open the doors

Anytime your power is off refrain from opening the refrigerator or freezer doors. After a storm you'll most likely want to have access to a few items. Prepare an ice chest before hand and once the power goes out, put the items you need into the ice chest. After you move items to the ice chest hopefully you won't have to open the refrigerator doors again.

4. Set the refrigerator and freezer to the coldest setting

When you're expecting a bad storm that will most likely result in a power outage, set your refrigerator and freezer to the coldest setting. The colder your appliance is before the power shuts off, the longer it will keep food cool.

Most importantly, if you doubt the safety of the food in any way, throw it out! Once perishable food reaches 40 degrees for longer than an hour or two, it is no longer safe to eat.

An indicator to know if your freezer food is safe is to fill a drink bottle half way with water. Lay it on it's side and freeze. When frozen stand the bottle upright again. If the power goes off for a long time while you're gone and the temp in the freezer warms up, the ice will melt and you'll know to toss the food. You can add a few drops of food coloring to make it more noticeable.

Bathe:

Winter storm warming? Severe thunderstorms heading your way? Enjoy a hot shower then wrangle the kids into the bathtub. It might be a couple of days before you have hot water. If needed, do the laundry too.

Clean:

If you are lucky enough to have warning a storm is coming, it's not essential really, but when you're stuck at home with no power, it's nice to at least not have dirty dishes staring you down while you can do nothing about them. You might like to run the dishwasher and vacuum in case you can't for a while.

Gas Up the Car:

Keep your car's tank at least 1/2 full at all times and keep a can of gas somewhere at home. If you don't have power, your local gas station may not either. Those pumps run on electricity these days. If your power will be out for several days, you may decide to evacuate to the home of a friend or family member until it's restored. You'll need enough gas to get there or at least enough to travel to an area that has open gas stations.

Don't Ruin Your TV:

When the power grid sputters back to life, it will probably create power surges which can destroy sensitive electronics in TVs, computers, and appliances. So unplug anything that may contain electronic components. Leave one light switched on to let you know when the power is restored. And if you have a generator, check the manual. Most inexpensive models churn out "dirty" power that can harm electronics.

Energy Back-Ups:

- generators
- chopped wood if you have a fireplace or fire pit
- filled grill tanks with propane
- extra fuel for camp stove

Keeping Warm:

- Sleeping bags zipped together keep two people warmer than in individual bags.
- Wear layers of clothing
- Wear hats, gloves, scarfs and socks. Body heat escapes from your head and feet.
- Avoid drinking cold water and beverages as this will require your body to heat it back up to your normal temperature, making your body work harder than it needs to.
- Live in one room, cover windows and doors with blankets to keep out the cold
- Open the drapes when the sun is shining on the windows
- Nothing warms the soul and the body quite like a hot cup of chicken noodle soup. While a propane cook stove won't heat the room it can heat up water for tea, hot chocolate or soup.
- Cuddle with your family. Sleeping together can help share body heat and protect smaller humans and the elderly who may not create enough heat themselves.
- Use a propane heater and wood burning fireplace.
- Be safe with a CO detector: Blackouts often lead to carbon monoxide deaths. Here's why: To get heat during outages, people crank up fireplaces, gas stoves, and all types of heaters and anything that burns produces carbon monoxide.

Keeping Cool:

During an extended power outage, heat can be more than just uncomfortable; it can be downright dangerous. Continued exposure to excessive heat can lead to hyperthermia and heat exhaustion. If left untreated, heat exhaustion can quickly progress to heat stroke and death, so early treatment and proactive cooling measures are extremely important.

- Close off the warmest rooms. If other rooms in your home are normally warmer than others be sure to close them off as much as possible to ensure that the hot air doesn't seep into the rest of the house
- Misting bottle
- Hand fan
- Battery operated fan
- Cooling scarf. For extra relief either indoors or outdoors, try a cooling scarf, it's a cloth scarf that contains a water absorbing gel, bringing hours of relief. It does require soaking the scarf prior to use.
- Stay out of the sun. Use an umbrella.
- Rung out wet sheets on the bed at night
- During the day, keep your shades drawn and your windows closed; or, if it's windy, hang lightweight linens that block solar rays, but still allow a light breeze to enter your home. Remember to wet them first.
- At night open the windows to let in the cooler air
- Wet t-shirts and bandannas
- Wear loose-fitting clothes
- Swimming
- Change your diet. Eat lighter meals with emphasis on vegetables and fruit instead of fatty foods.
- Stay hydrated. Keep your water intake up to keep yourself cool. Avoid alcoholic and caffeinated drinks when out in the heat, they increase the risk of dehydration.
- Don't forget your pets can get overheated as well, so make sure you give them plenty of water and shade as well.

Portable Radio:

Lets you listen for weather or emergency information anywhere. Some models have a solar panel or a hand crank for recharging, so you don't even need batteries.

Additional Emergency Preparations:

First Aid Kit

If you haven't already, I highly recommend taking a course in first aid. Otherwise, all of these supplies will be pretty much useless in a true emergency situation. Learn skills like how to dress a wound, CPR, how to set a splint, and which medications to give.

Buy a proper first aid kit which fits the needs of your family. Add to it the remedies you normally use such as essential oils, herbal, homeopathic, or other natural remedies you know how to use.

Don't forget the q-tips, tweezers, nail clippers, small scissors, thermometer, extra band-aids, butterfly strips, super glue, lots of gloves, hand sanitizer, face masks, eye drops, hydrogen peroxide.

We usually have most of these things in our home but maybe not all in one place. To avoid precious time and confusion trying to find things in an actual emergency, gather your first aid items and keep them together in one place. This also allows you to quickly grab them in case you had to leave the house quickly.

Financial

Prioritize the most likely emergencies first. Medical issues and financial difficulties are the most likely disruptions you'll face in your lifetime.

All of the statistics around personal financial health are shockingly bad, particularly in the US. For example, over 50% of

Americans can't handle an unexpected $500 emergency (eg. your expired-warranty home furnace suddenly fails) without using credit cards.

You should not spend any money on gear/supplies beyond the essentials (eg. two weeks of water in your home) without first having core financial preps such as a rainy day fund, debt-reduction plan, and retirement savings. Don't forget other basics like insurance and estate planning. Do you have a will? Does your family know what to do if you're in a bad accident and can't talk? Do you want doctors to keep you alive in a vegetative coma? Have you added beneficiaries to your financial accounts so your family isn't locked out from money while waiting for the probate court system?

Documents

- copy of deeds/titles
- insurance policies
- birth certificates
- maps
- pictures of family members, etc. in both physical and USB thumb drive forms
- old school address book with phone numbers in case you don't have access to your cell phone

Cash

- as much as you can reasonably afford to stash

Tools

- axe
- shovel
- work gloves
- wrench for your gas lines

- zip ties
- duct tape, etc.

Light

- headlamps
- flashlights
- candles
- lanterns
- solar outdoor lights
- glow sticks

Fire

- lighters
- matches
- backup fire starters

Mental Health

- board games
- favorite books
- headphones
- movies downloaded to a tablet, etc.

Self Defense

- Weapons, pepper spray, etc.
- Hidden cash and/or credit cards
- In Case of Emergency details (eg. a laminated card of important info kept in a wallet)
- Phone (usually with downloaded maps and helpful apps)
- Lithium-Ion rechargeable battery pack
- Flashlight
- Pocket knife

- Multitool
- Lighter

Emergency Gear Kept In The Car

If you have a vehicle, you should keep basic gear on hand for road-related emergencies. These items don't need to be kept in a backpack since it's very unlikely you'll need to carry them on foot over distance.

- In Case of Emergency info kept in a glove box or console
- Maps
- Window breaker and seatbelt cutter tool
- Mylar emergency blanket 1-2x
- Proper blanket or extra coat
- Extra hat, sunglasses, sunscreen
- Jump start battery
- Jumper cables
- Tow straps
- Road flares or blaze signal
- Spare tire
- Tire wrench
- Jack
- Tire repair kit (plug holes instead of replace the whole tire)
- Windshield scraper
- Deicing wiper fluid
- A small shovel (ie. "e-tool" or entrenching tool) or garden trowel for digging out tires
- Kitty litter, sand, or other spreadable traction
- Traction boards
- Boo-boo kit, IFAK, Rx meds, extra glasses, etc.
- Plug to turn a cigarette lighter into a USB charger
- Stored water and/or water filter

Further Preparations:

- How you progress from here starts to greatly depend on your goals and circumstances. Roughly speaking, people tend to:
- Increase the amount of time they can survive in their home without the help or grid, which usually means increasing supplies (eg. having multiple months of food and water) and improving the home so it doesn't need the grid.
- Get into more advanced gear, such as hunting, fishing and firearms,
- Explore ways to create their own food through farming or livestock, even if it's a small indoor garden, backyard chickens or meat rabbits.
- Explore ways to capture their own water via rain collection systems, etc.
- Buy or build a bug out vehicle.
- Be more intentional about cooking at home, repairing or mending products, composting, and other general homesteading techniques.
- Build up a resource library of survival books or other info not dependent on the internet.
- Continue improving their physical fitness and personal finances.
- Hedge against economic risks with precious metals and/ or cryptocurrency.
- Build or buy a bug out location, such as a cabin in the woods a reasonable drive away from home.
- Continue learning advanced skills, such as plant medicine, first aid, homesteading skills or carpentry.

It's the old-fashioned basics of self-reliance, self-motivation, self-reinforcement, self-discipline, and self-command that will allow you to face challenges with confidence and peace of mind.

CHAPTER 23

Pets in a Disaster

There's not much time to react when disaster strikes, especially when it's a life or death situation. You want to get out safely and as soon as possible with your family, and that includes your pets.

Saving your pets comes with its own set of circumstances, however. For instance, many evacuation centers, should you be displaced there, don't allow pets. So what do you do? Here's the best course of action to protect your human and four-legged loved ones, should you need to evacuate your home quickly.

Create An Emergency Bag For Your Pet

You should have an emergency bag for yourself and your family, but you also should have a separate bag for your pet to ensure that everyone's needs are covered for at least the first few days following a disaster. Your pet's bag should include:

- At least three days worth of food and water, plus portable bowls.

- Vet records from the previous two years, including vaccinations, your pet's microchip number, medications, and any allergies. Be sure to have a supply of your pet's meds packed as well.
- First-aid kit for pets; the Red Cross provides a comprehensive list of what you should have if you want to DIY (if you have a first aid kit already, there are several items that will also work for your pets), but you also can buy one online.
- Muzzle if your animal has a tendency to be aggressive, especially when frightened.
- Pet carrier.
- Put favorite toys, treats or bedding in your pets bag. Familiar items can help reduce stress for your pet.
- Treats to calm your pets.
- Photo of you with your pet to assist search and rescue should it go missing.
- Collar with ID and rabies tags.
- Your vet's phone number, in case of emergency.
- Waste bags.
- Extra litter and a spare litter box if you're a cat owner.

Take Pet CPR And First-Aid Classes

In the event of a disaster, your dog or cat can break limbs or incur wounds with serious bleeding, and knowing how to respond appropriately in that moment can mean the difference between life and death.

A good pet CPR class will teach you how to properly administer chest compressions and rescue breathing, create improvised splints for securing broken bones, how to perform basic wound care and stop life-threatening bleeding, and give you a list of items for your pet first aid kit.

Training

The first thing to do to protect your dog is to ensure that it will obey your commands when it matters most, in emergencies. For starters, "stay" is an important thing to teach. It seems like most owners find teaching this command a challenge, so brushing up on it is always a good idea. It's also useful to train your dog to bark, be quiet, refuse food from strangers, and carry their bug out bag.

Get Your Pet Micro-Chipped

Your pet should be micro-chipped when it's spayed or neutered, but if it hasn't been, have the chip put in your pet as soon as possible. A microchip is implanted between your pet's shoulders and is about the size of a grain of rice. The procedure itself is similar to a pet getting a vaccine. The information on the chip will go to a database after it's registered (an important step that some pet parents overlook) and scanned that will include your pet's number and profile, along with your contact information. You may never have to use the chip, but when a lost pet is brought into a vet's office or shelter, the first thing they do is scan for a microchip, so if your pet has one, there's a much better chance you'll be reunited should you get split up.

Put A GPS Tracker On Your Pet

A reliable pet GPS tracker also makes it possible to keep track of pets during an emergency. The lightweight, waterproof device attaches comfortably to your pet's collar or harness, and allows you to track your pet's location anywhere in the U.S. The battery on these typically lasts several days, providing an ample window to find your pet in the event you're separated during a disaster.

Affix A Pet Alert Sticker To Your Window

In case of emergency, first-responders will be able to identify your household as one that may need pets rescued with a pet alert sticker placed where it can be clearly seen. Write down the number of pets inside your house and attach to a front window.

Have An Exit Strategy

Leaving your pet's carrier and emergency go bag by the door so you can access it quickly and easily in the event that you have to leave in a split second.

Evacuate Early

Don't wait for a mandatory evacuation order. Some people who have waited to be evacuated by emergency officials have been told to leave their pets behind. The smell of smoke or the sound of high winds or thunder may make your pet more fearful and difficult to load into a crate or carrier. Evacuating before conditions become severe will keep everyone safer and make the process less stressful.

Never Leave Your Pets Behind

Your pet is a member of your family, and should be treated as such when you're evacuating. Don't leave your animal in vehicles, tethered, or crated without you or a family member.

To help avoid having to make such a difficult choice, identify and create a list of places to evacuate with your pets in preparation, such as pet-friendly hotels or boarding facilities, and include contact information and addresses for each.

Large Animals

Large animals and livestock need extra consideration in disaster planning. Disaster preparedness is important for all animals, but it is especially important for livestock because of the size of the animals and their shelter and transportation needs.

Birds

Don't forget your birds, their food and traveling cages.

If You Stay Home, Do It Safely

If your family and pets must wait out a storm or other disaster at home, identify a safe area of your home where you can all stay together.

- Close off or eliminate unsafe nooks and crannies where frightened cats may try to hide.
- Move dangerous items such as tools or toxic products that have been stored in the area.
- Bring your pets indoors as soon as local authorities say trouble is on the way.
- Keep dogs on leashes and cats in carriers, and make sure they are wearing identification.
- If you have a room you can designate as a "safe room," put your emergency supplies in that room in advance, including your pet's crate and supplies. Have any medications and a supply of pet food and water inside

watertight containers, along with your other emergency supplies.

- If there is an open fireplace, vent, pet door or similar opening in the house, close it off with plastic sheeting and strong tape.
- Follow local news outlets online or listen to the radio periodically, and don't come out until you know it's safe.

Stay Healthy And Fit

The healthier and more fit you are on a normal day, the better chance you have staying that way during an emergency. Make good health choices for both you and your pets by eating healthy and staying active. Just remember an obese dog will be much harder to transport during an evacuation than a fit one. And you'll be much more able to deal with the emotional and physical stress if you're healthy too.

Even if you can't get to the gym every day, get out and go on long walks with your dog regularly. It's a great bonding experience and you'll be glad you did in the event of a natural disaster.

Include Your Pets In Your Will

So your pet is properly cared for when you pass away, in a disaster or otherwise, include those provisions in your will. Keep the information up-to-date with the names of each pet, the person who has agreed to care for the pet, and their contact information. If you want to provide that person money to care for the pet, state that in the will.

CHAPTER 24

Neighbors and Community

'Do we not realize that self-respect comes with self-reliance." Adul Kalam

Our neighbors are our village. A neighborhood is a street, an apartment complex or other area where people live. The people make it a neighborhood.

When a big disaster hits, life gets local, really quickly. So your neighbors are what you have to work with.

Before an emergency or disaster occurs you need to make an effort to get to know your neighbors. You may know the folks on either side of you and across the street but what about the people several houses down or a few blocks away? Do you know your neighbors?

When disaster strikes the reality is first responders will not be able to help everyone. Luckily, with some prior planning, you and your neighbors can help. It is the personal ties among members of a community that determine survival during a disaster, and recovery in its aftermath.

Whether you are new to your neighborhood or have lived there for 25 years, knowing your neighbors has always been an important part of a healthy community. During a crisis, it becomes invaluable because, after a disaster occurs, it's the people closest to you who can help most immediately.

It is well documented that when neighborhoods that are prepared for emergencies and disaster situations can save lives, reduce the severity of injuries, and minimize property damage. Working together as a team improves quality of life within a community.

Many people will say they already know their neighbors, but it makes a huge difference when neighbors share important contact information, when they add their neighbors as cell phone contacts for quick responses to emergencies and when they get together regularly to plan and practice what they'll do to help each other in an emergency, BEFORE it happens.

Many of us in America don't even know our neighbors. Changing that will help save lives in the event of a disaster, but it also enriches your life, even if Mother Nature doesn't strike. Become a community builder.

How To Get To Know Neighbors:

- When going outside to get the mail from your mailbox, greet, wave or say hello to your neighbors.
- Plan an outdoor neighborhood movie night.
- Invite friends over to play card games, make crafts or outdoor games in the yard.
- Plan a potluck dinner and have people bring their favorite recipe to share.
- Have a neighborhood yard sale.
- Hang out on your porch or in your front yard. It's hard to get to know your neighbors if you don't ever see them. Just by being out in front of your house you can give off a welcoming vibe that encourages interaction.

- Put up a Book Lending Cupboard. Take a book, lend a book. Collect your old reads and share them with passersby in a book-lending cupboard mounted next to the sidewalk out front. Give it a roof, a door with glass panes.
- Suggest having a girl's night out or a luncheon to get to know each other.
- If you see a garage door open that is usually not open (at night)….knock on the door of that home or call them if you know their phone number. I am sure they will be thankful to know it was open.
- Plan a "Clean up our street"….let your neighbors know about neighbors who could use a little help. They might be old and are hesitant to ask for help.
- Start up a community garden space and teach your neighbors how to grow their own food. This is a time-tested way to promote community interaction in your neighborhood as well as share in a bounty of fresh veggies.
- If you have kids plan play dates, join the local PTA or volunteer to coach a youth team.
- If you feel comfortable, ask neighbors for family members' phone numbers you can contact in case of an emergency. Let them know of any special talents/skills you have that might come in handy.
- Throw a neighborhood "disaster planning"party, inviting your neighbors, in a jovial and relaxed environment, finding out what skills people have, and what "stuff" they've got. If one guy has a chainsaw, that's plenty. The whole neighborhood doesn't need a chainsaw. Knowing that one neighbor used to be in the Army and another was a lifeguard can help if you're searching for help.
- Have you ever thought about a block party? Suggest a park or area close by so people can exchange ideas about what you have available to help each other survive a

disaster. Some people have no idea they should store water, food, etc.

- Get a dog. Not only can they alarm you in an emergency, it is wonderful to take a dog walking and meet neighbors.
- If you make bread take a loaf to a neighbor. Exchange phone numbers so you have someone you can contact if help is needed in a real emergency or disaster.
- Have a barbecue in the front yard and send notes around to neighbors to bring a dish and their own meat of choice. Chairs are welcome too!
- Spend more time in the front yard, porch or balcony. Say hi to those who pass by on foot, riding their bike, etc.
- Host a porch party. I love hanging out on my front porch, and a porch party feels like an easy way to socialize with your neighbors without the work of a "real" party.
- Make a jar of jam or something and deliver to neighbors with your name and contact information on an attached tag. Indicate you are available in case they need help.
- Welcome new families. You can bring a traditional baked good, but I also love the idea of welcoming newcomers by sharing your favorite local restaurants and businesses, perhaps a stack of your favorite take-out menus wrapped up in ribbon.
- Share small neighborhood gifts at holiday times. It's rare that anyone gets anything fun in the mail these days. Why not surprise your neighbor with a holiday treat? Keep it simple…baked goods, seasoned popcorn, nuts, candy.
- Let your neighbors know when you will be out of town and ask them to contact you or the police if anything is suspicious. You don't need a formalized neighborhood watch program to keep the neighborhood safe. If you ask your neighbors, they will likely ask you in turn, which helps to keep the neighborhood safe for everyone.

Disaster Response Involves Everyone

Being prepared can feel overwhelming, but you don't have to have it all figured out. Just focus on one aspect at a time. Being even a little prepared is better than not being prepared at all. If you aren't ready to launch a neighborhood group, start by simply getting to know your neighbors better. Research shows that people who know and trust their neighbors are more likely to report higher rates of health and well-being than those who do not. And don't forget, it's a lot easier to ask to borrow an organic onion, or whatever it is that you are out of while making dinner, if you already know your neighbor.

Disaster response involves everyone. The better prepared you are, the better you can help yourself and others. It's never too late to get to know your neighbors.

Resources:

There are endless online resources about preparedness:
- 'Map Your Neighborhood' can be a good resource. This website has links to many things you can use to organize your neighborhood, including step-by-step planning, worksheets and a series of videos. islandcountywa.gov/ DEM/Pages/Map-Your-Neighborhood.aspx
- Ready.gov has all the resources you need to make individual, family and neighborhood planning. www. ready.gov/plan

Look for organizations who specialize in natural disasters most likely to occur in your area; floods, earthquakes, hurricanes, etc.

CONCLUSION

Nothing destroys the individuality of a woman as much as the failure to be self-reliant. Every woman has a mysterious force within her, an ancient wisdom that is always whispering. She has a divine holy force that has been contained and restricted for millennia but is ready to rise again.

Self-reliance is the way of the Divine Feminine. Relying on others brings failure maximum times as history proves. Divine Feminine self-reliance guarantees success in resurrecting the values once associated with female-based religious systems:

- values of kindness
- compassion and healing
- of providing and sheltering
- of nourishing and protecting
- of holding all life sacred to include the earth, all living creatures and the plant kingdom
- and most of all, love for humanity

From the dawn of prehistory, women were perceived as holy, sacred, and divine incarnations of the Great Mother Goddess. Powerful figures full of strength, wisdom, and leadership, women were the keepers of the human race, from which all life flowed. To be these things you have to be self-reliant and prepared for feasts and famines and everything in-between. Modern life is making us vulnerable, dependent, needy and lazy.

You are a Divine Feminine. You come from a long lineage of Divine self-reliant woman who began the world. It is your destiny and in your DNA to persevere, be strong and overcome challenges. These are our roots, we modern contemporary women, all of us, from all walks of life, are reflections and descendants of the ancient Divine Feminine.

Although we still have a long way to go, women have more control today than ever before over their careers, bodies, finances, and lifestyles. Women are capable of supporting themselves and their families and are breaking old stereotypes of traditional weak female roles. A strong, independent woman doesn't need to try to fit into a certain mold that our patriarchal society has created. Now is the time to unleash your Inner Goddess, be self-confident, self-reliant and practice extreme self-care.

The world needs women to wake up their Divine Feminine Power. Collectively, we will intentionally bring back Divine Feminine Energy to balance out our troubled world. This is no easy task but living on this earth never has been.

Whenever we get into situations which threaten our self-reliance, we will find our freedoms threatened as well. If we increase our dependence on anything or anyone we will find an immediate decrease in our freedom to act.

The Divine Feminine is sometimes referred to as the "Sacred Feminine" or the "Goddess." The Goddess is the feminine aspect of the Divine, of humanity, of life, and of creation itself. As women, we are its expression and representation; we are an extension and a reflection of this feminine energy.

Likewise, men are an expression of the masculine aspect of the Divine. We see greed, disruption, and hate around us because we have been living in a world where the feminine has been subjugated, denounced, and neither honored nor respected for centuries. Without its true counterpart next to it in perfect balance and harmony, what we see is the distorted, twisted, and unbalanced masculine aspect. This unbalanced masculine aspect is unable to show itself as the Divine Masculine without its feminine counterpart to balance it.

The time has come to rise up and balance the scales and return to the Divine Feminine by being kind, loving, accepting, and forgiving of yourself and other humans. While our goals may be idealistic we must also be realistic about the state of our troubled world and our uncertain future, on many levels.

It is our divine responsibility to be self-reliant and prepared for what may come and what is already here; wildfires, drought, floods, extreme hot and cold weather, power outages, food shortages, impending claimant change, dollar devaluation, supply chain failures, local and global pandemic, water contamination, civil unrest, etc.

As our modern systems continue to fail us it's all likely to get worse. You can rise up and stare adversity and disaster in the eyes when you are a prepared, self-reliant Warrior Goddess with a fiery spirit and a strong heart.

Today is your wake up call to be the strong self-reliant Divine Feminine you are meant to be. You are strong enough to get up, step up and start remembering the magic and dreams you have inside of yourself. And so it is.

RESOURCES & REFERENCES

Back to Eden (gardening), Paul Gautschi
Back to Eden (natural living), Jethro Kloss
Fermented Vegetables, Kirsten and Christopher Shockey
From Scratch by Shaye Elliott of the Elliott Homestead
Grow Your Own Tea, Christine Parks & Susan M. Walcote
Just Grow It Yourself, David G. Fisher
Kiss The Ground, documentary
Make Mead Like a Viking, Jereme Zimmerman
Nourishing Traditions Cookbook by Sally Fallon
Nourishing Traditions: The Cookbook that Challenges Politically
Correct Nutrition and the Diet Dictocrats by Sally Fallon and
Mary Enig.
Super Loaves & Simple Treats, Melissa Sharp
Sprouts the Master Food, Steve Meyerowitz
Square Foot Gardening, Mel Bartholomew
The Art of Fermentation, Sandor Ellix Katz
The Big Book of Kombucha, Hannah Crum
The Dehydrator Bible, Jennifer MacKenzie
The Kimchi Diet, Dr. Susanne Bennett
Wild Fermentation, Sandor Ellix Katz

ABOUT THE AUTHOR

Marilyn Pabon has a keen insight and understanding of the physical and spiritual aspects of being a woman. She spent over 20 years researching and practicing holistic nutrition, energy healing and all things related to natural wellness. She has always been a spiritual seeker, very intuitive, and has the gift of a very thin veil between this world and the spirit world.

While studying Shamanism and learning the first Shaman were women, led her to learn all she could about the history of women to include prehistoric women. During this research she had an awakening as to the divinity of women, especially the ancient divine feminine who began the world and how their energy has returned to the earth to bring balance and healing to the world. This knowledge, research, and training over the years came to a full circle of understanding the big beautiful picture of the purpose of modern divine feminine women.

Marilyn's mission is to empower women to find the path back to their souls and their divinity by guiding them toward self-love and inner transformation. She has written a four-book series "Divine Feminine Handbook" to teach women their divine history, who they really are, their specialness, how to love themselves, have self-confidence, carry themselves like a goddess, care for their physical temples and be self-reliant.

Marilyn is a California native currently living in Utah's beautiful red rock country at the gateway to Zion National Park with her husband and daughter. For more information about her work and books, visit: www.marilynpabon.com

SHARE THE DREAM

Divine Feminine Handbook I, II, III, and IV are more than a set of books.

It is a lifestyle and movement in which modern women can live to their greatest and truest versions of themselves. It's a dedication to empower women to break free from the shackles of outdated and limiting beliefs. It is a call to awaken the Divine Feminine Energy in us all. It is a remembrance of our divine ancient foremothers who were once revered as creators of life, healers, spiritual guides, shamans and leaders.

If you too have a dream of helping your divine sisters learn of their sacred heritage and cultivate their goddess within, so they too can live empowered fulfilling lives, please share these books.

One of the simplest ways you can do that is by leaving a review online. Write down your thoughts about the book on your favorite book selling or review sites so that other Divine Feminine women can be inspired to know more.

You can also share your ideas on your social media page. Make sure to include the official hashtag: #divinefemininehandbooks.

From my heart to yours,
Marilyn Pabon

MESSAGE FROM THE AUTHOR

It has been my honor to share the history, journey and return of the Divine Feminine on Mother Earth at this time. I am a life long student, seeker and researcher. I consider myself a steward of information which I felt inspired to share and pass on in the form of the Divine Feminine Handbooks.

I am eternally grateful for the wonderful teachers, leaders and authors who I have either trained, worked and studied with or read their works. Everything I know has been learned from many others who have blazed the trail before me. I have condensed many years of study and prayer into four volumes for you to learn many subjects much quicker than it took me.

My advise to you is to stay curious. Being curious means you look forward to learning new things and are troubled by gaps in your understanding of the world. New words and ideas are received as challenges, and the work of understanding them is embraced. People who lack curiosity see learning new things as a chore or worse, as beyond their capacities and will likely shy away from becoming self-taught. Never stop learning. Our knowledge and experiences in this life are what we take with us to the next life.

My gift to you is for you to remember who you are, the history of where you came from, the divine that is within you and your infinite Divine Feminine potential. You are a wise soul with all the wisdom and tools you needed to come to this earth. Your spiritual nature is self-reliant, strong and independent or you wouldn't be here. You are born into this world alone and you leave this world alone as you go back to the spirit world from whence you came, as though waking from a dream. You take with you your memories, stories, experiences, and the earthly knowledge you gained while here.

It is my hope you will return victorious as a warrior goddess who conquered her fears and contributed to the betterment of the world.

Printed in the United States
by Baker & Taylor Publisher Services